COLORING ADVENTURE
KITTY KAIJU

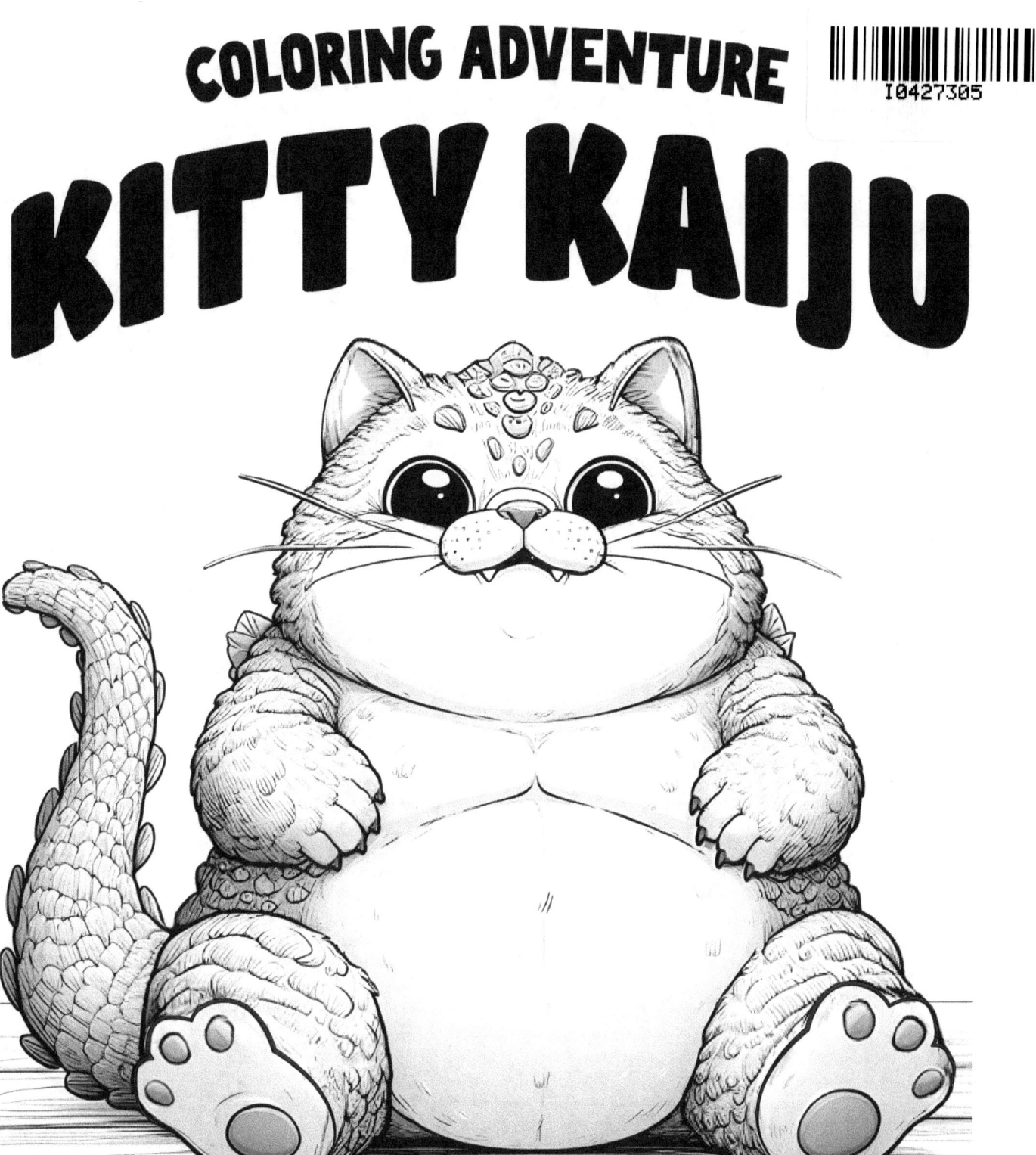

COLORING BOOK

BY CHASE KAIHUS

Dive into the Whimsical World of Cat Monster Kaijus
Perfect for Stress Relief - Perfect for Relaxation and Fun!

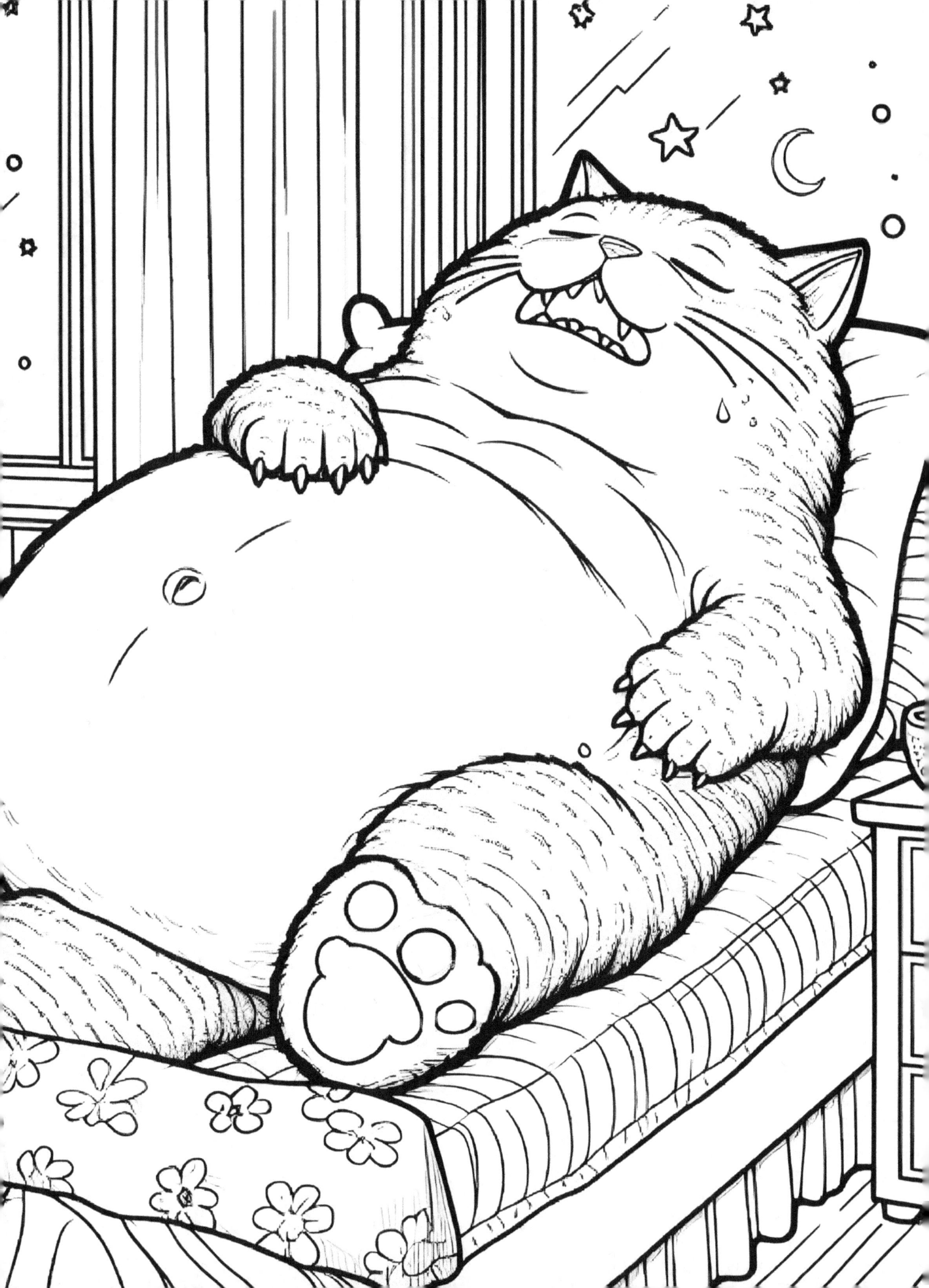

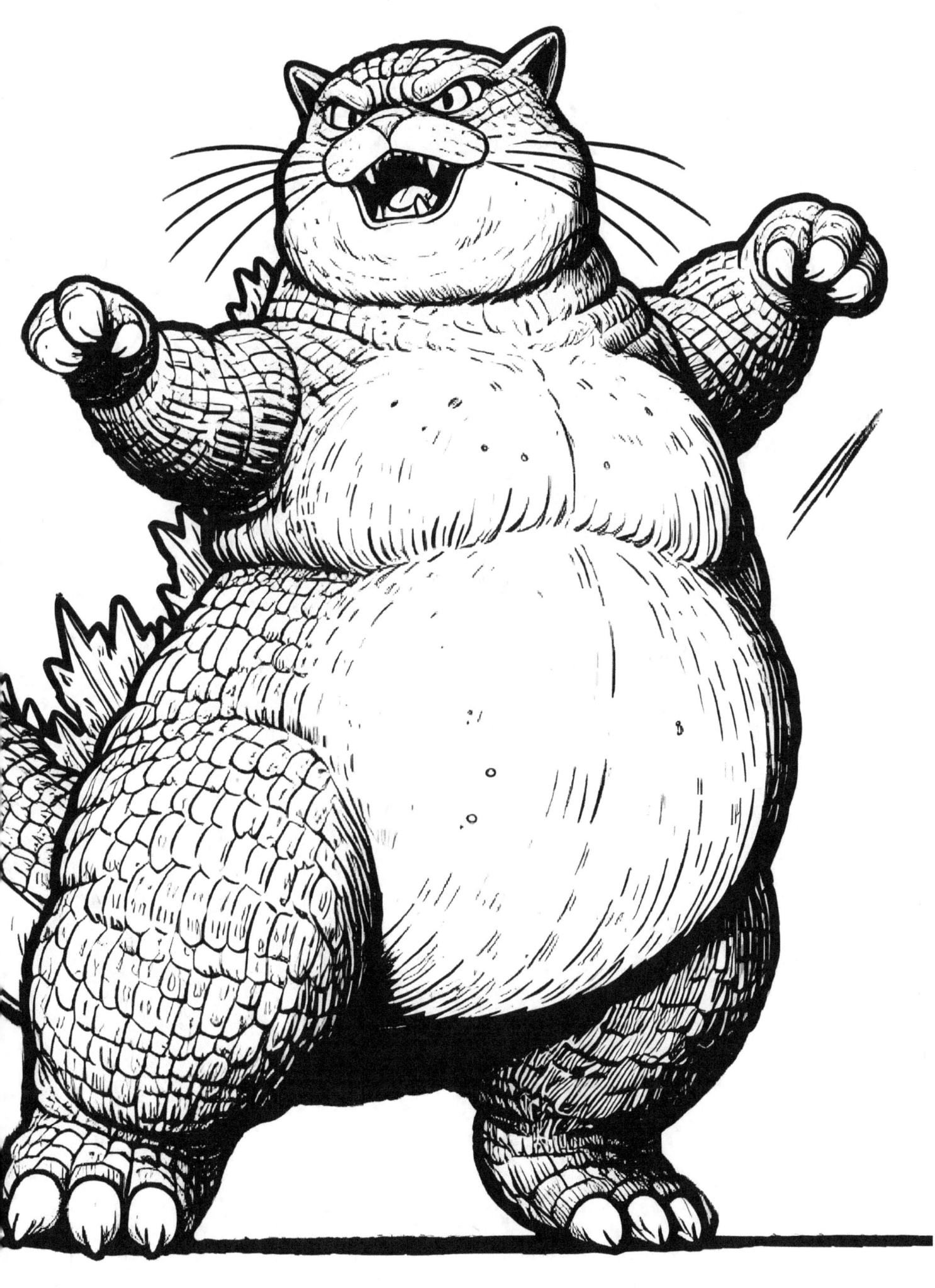

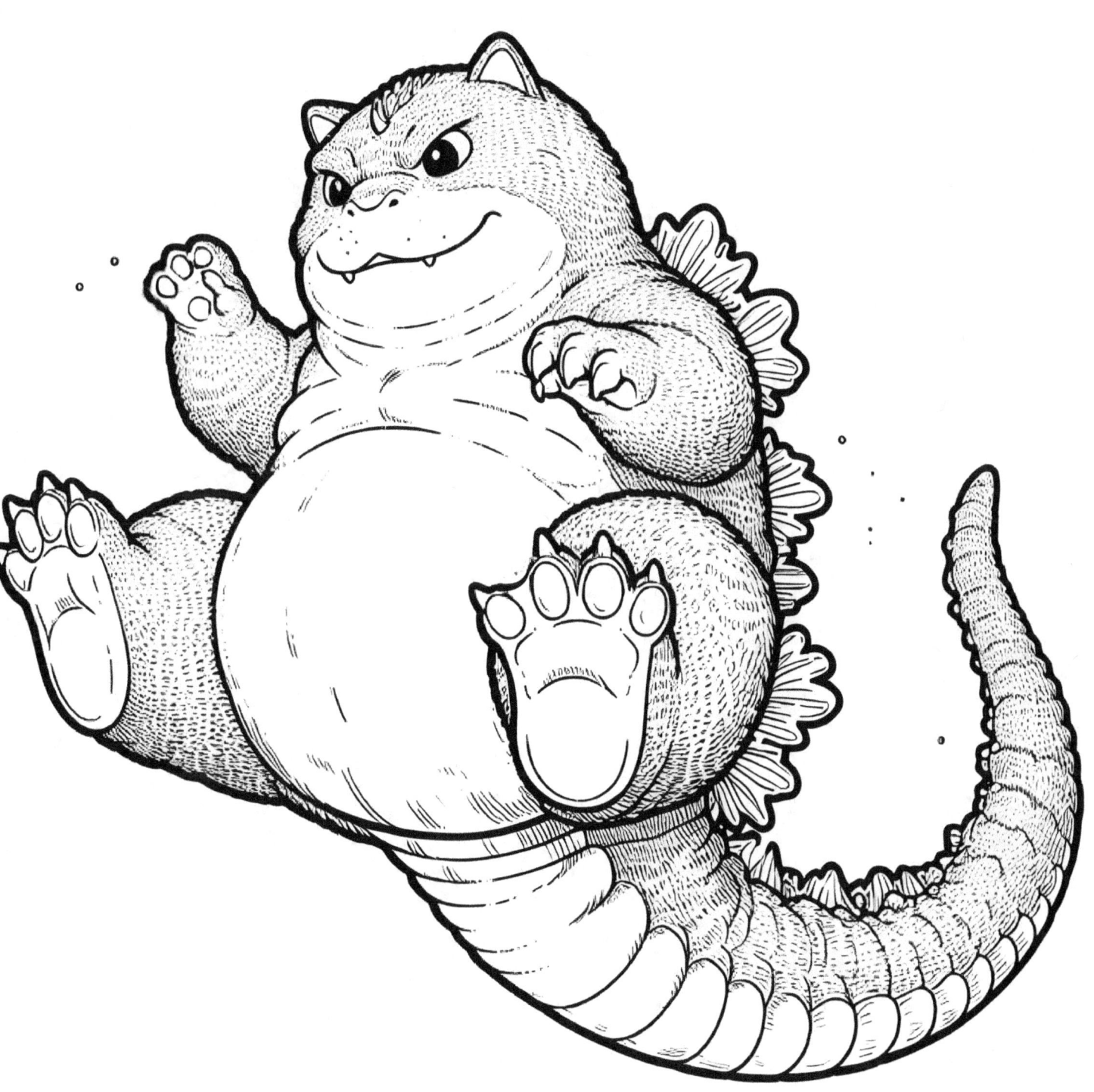

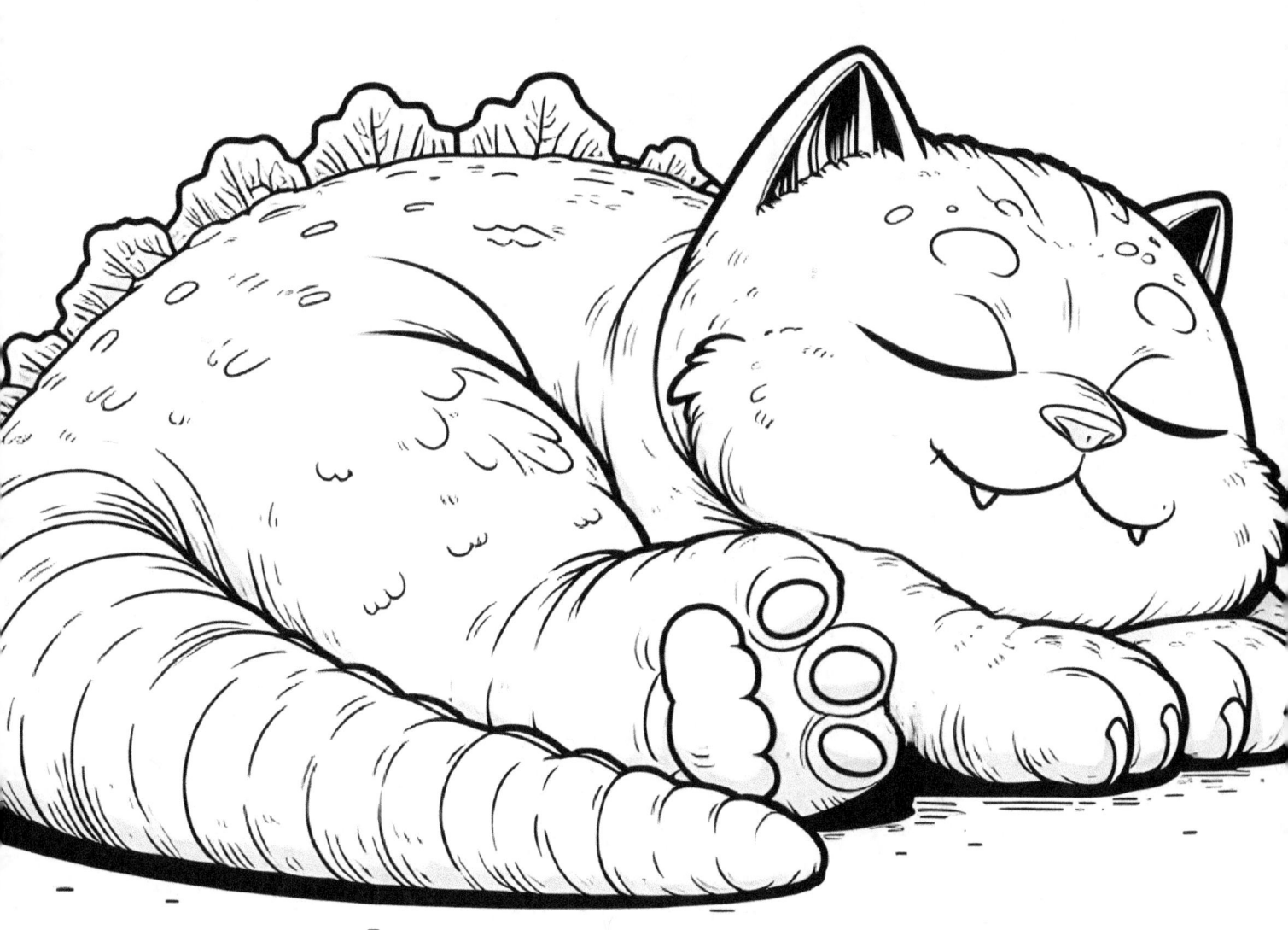

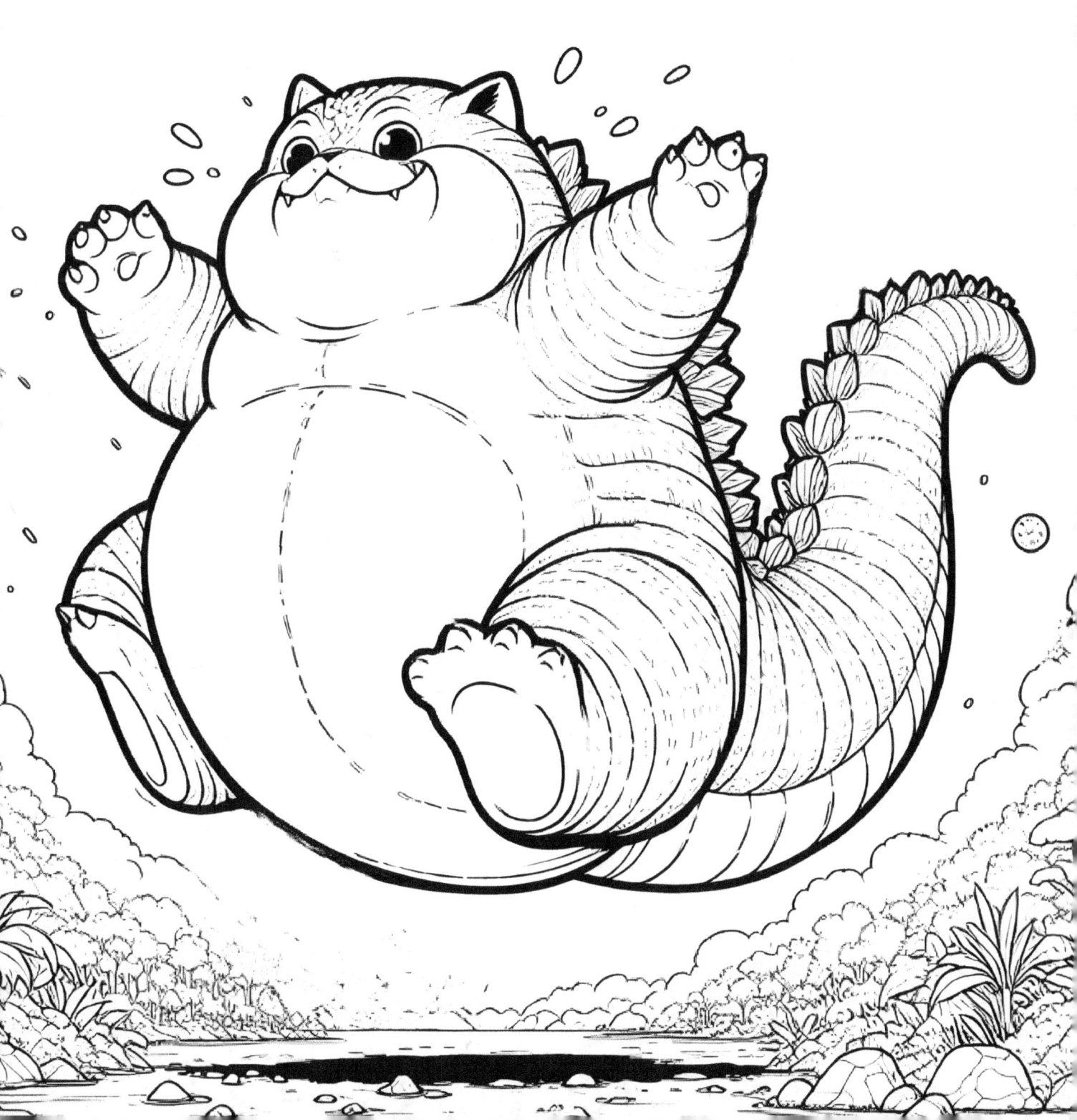

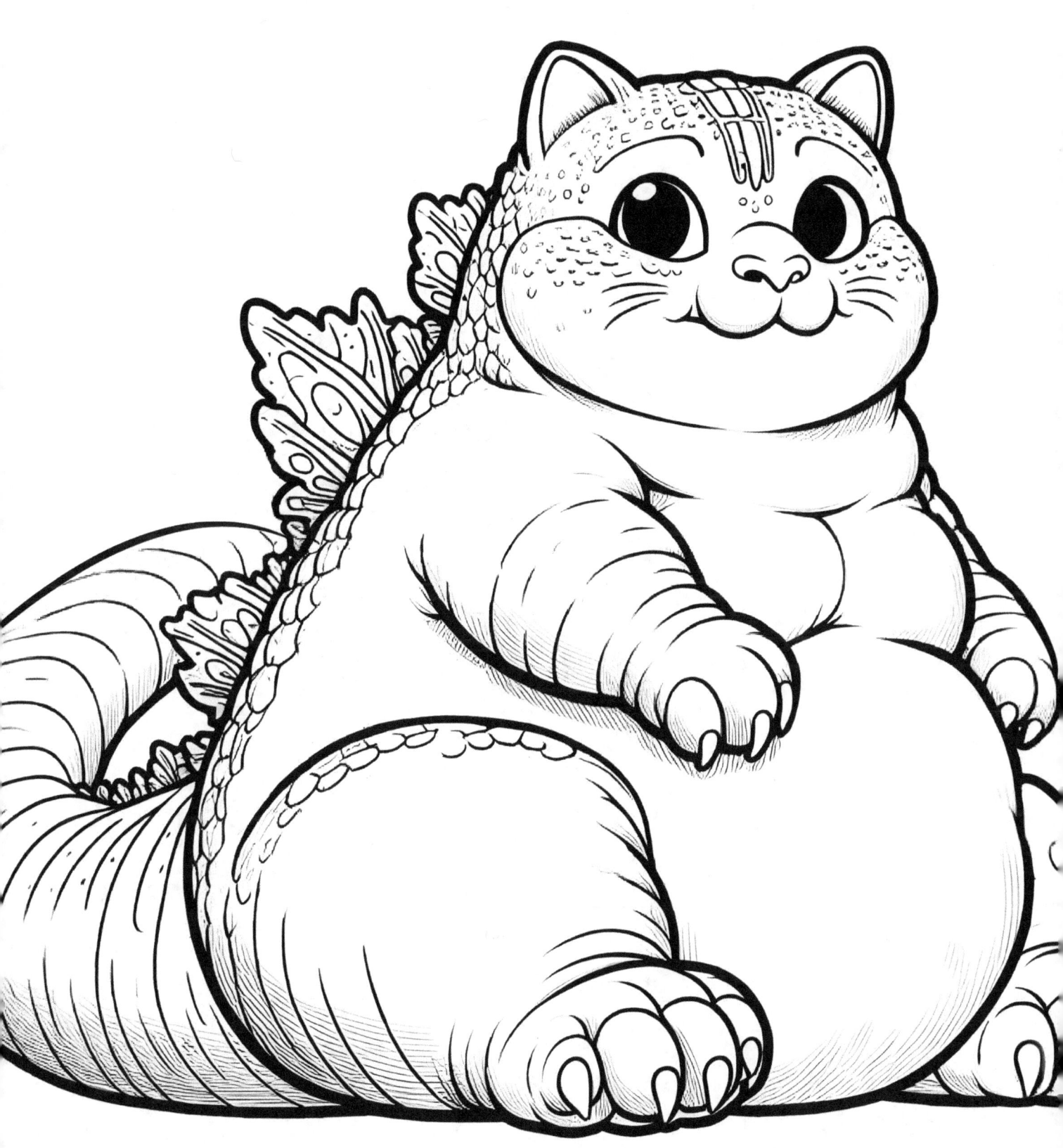

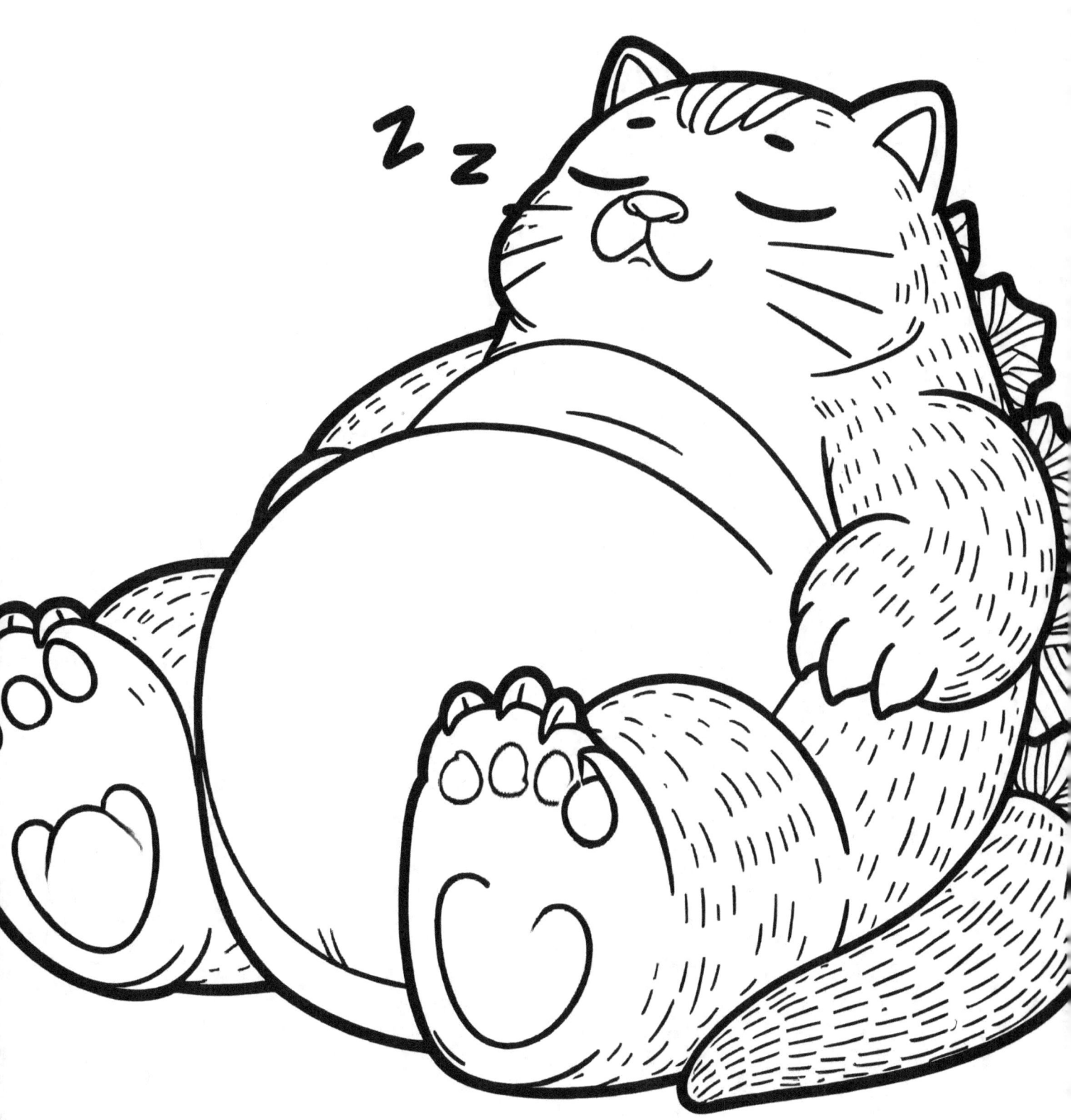

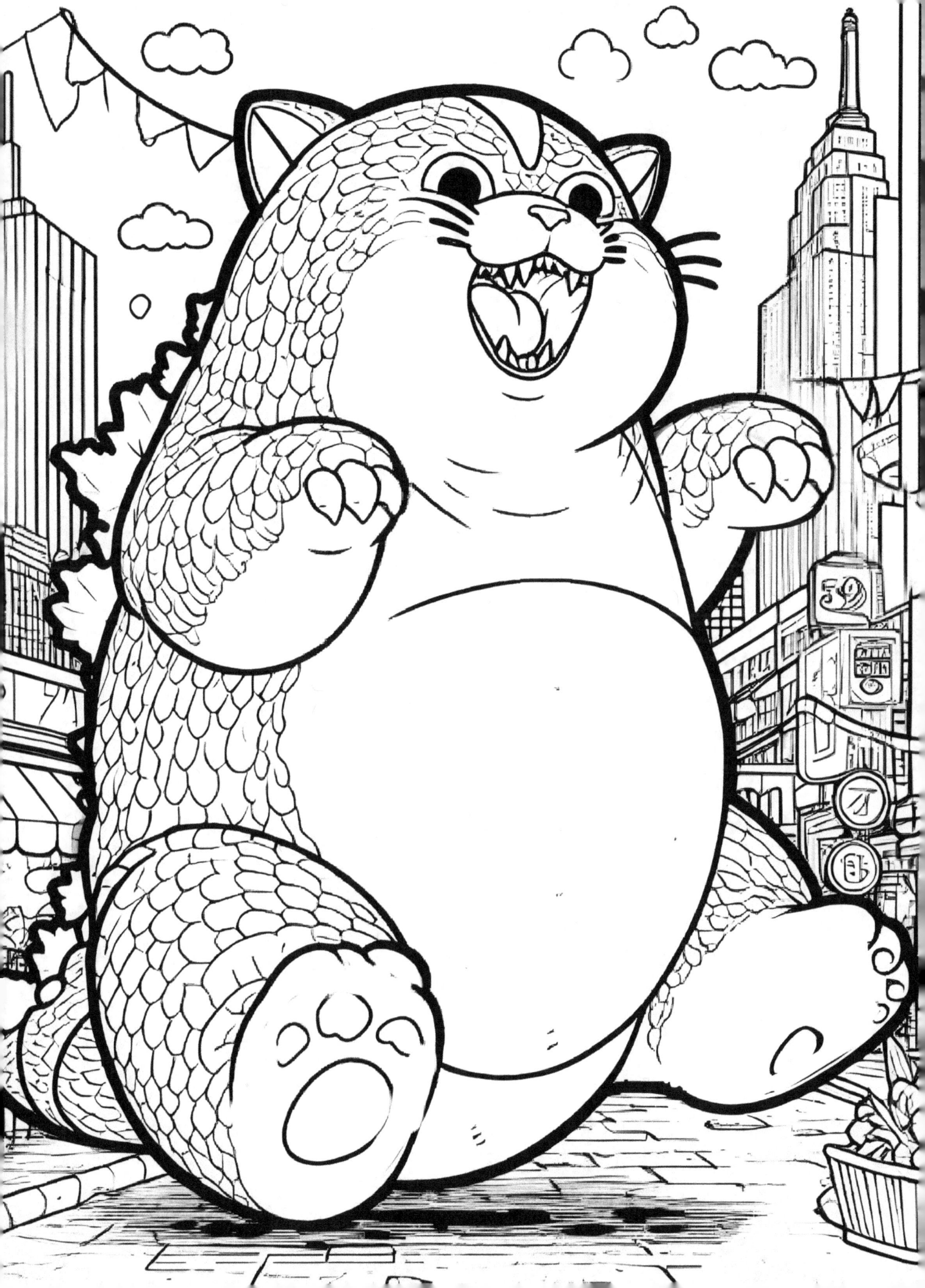

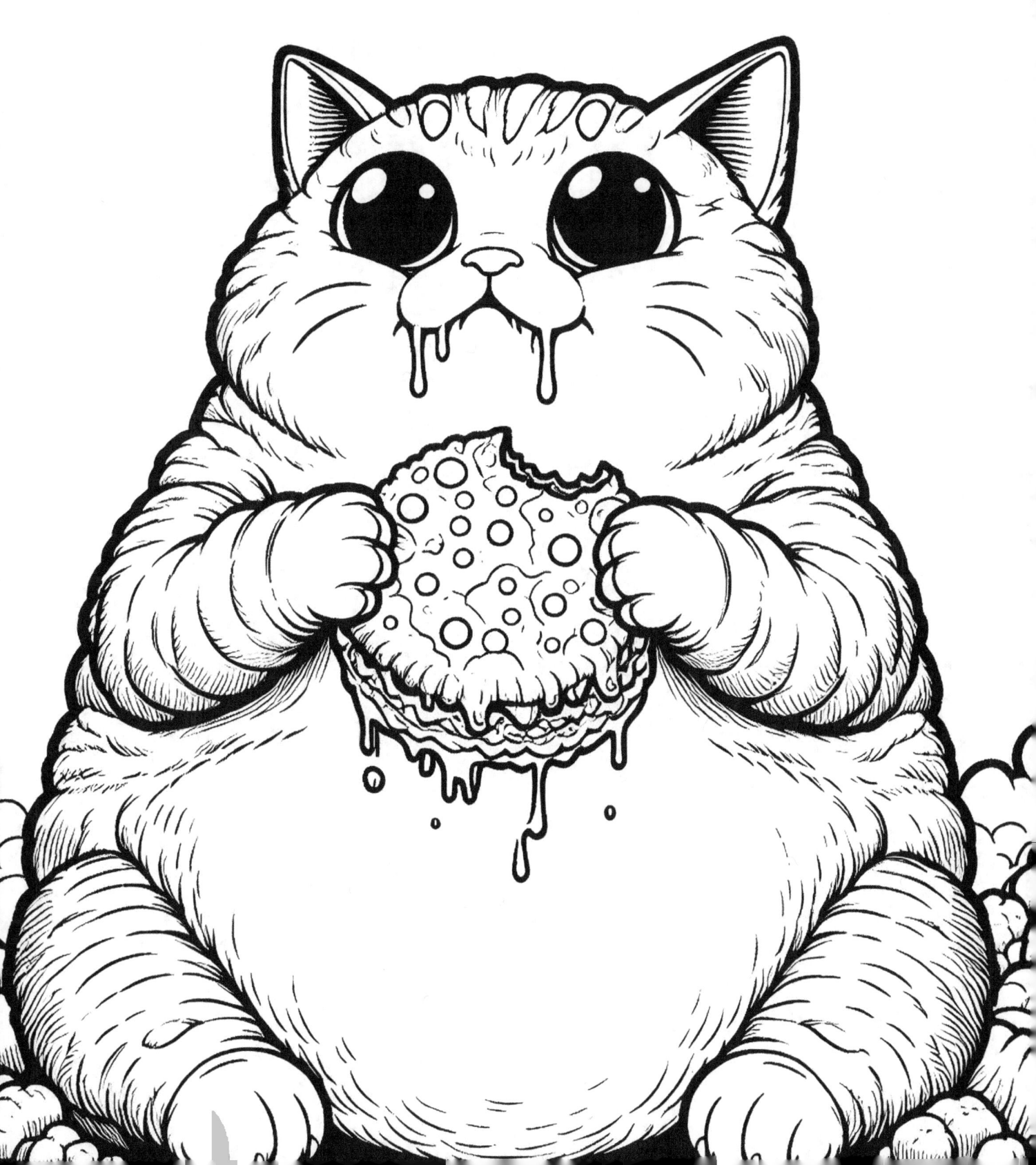

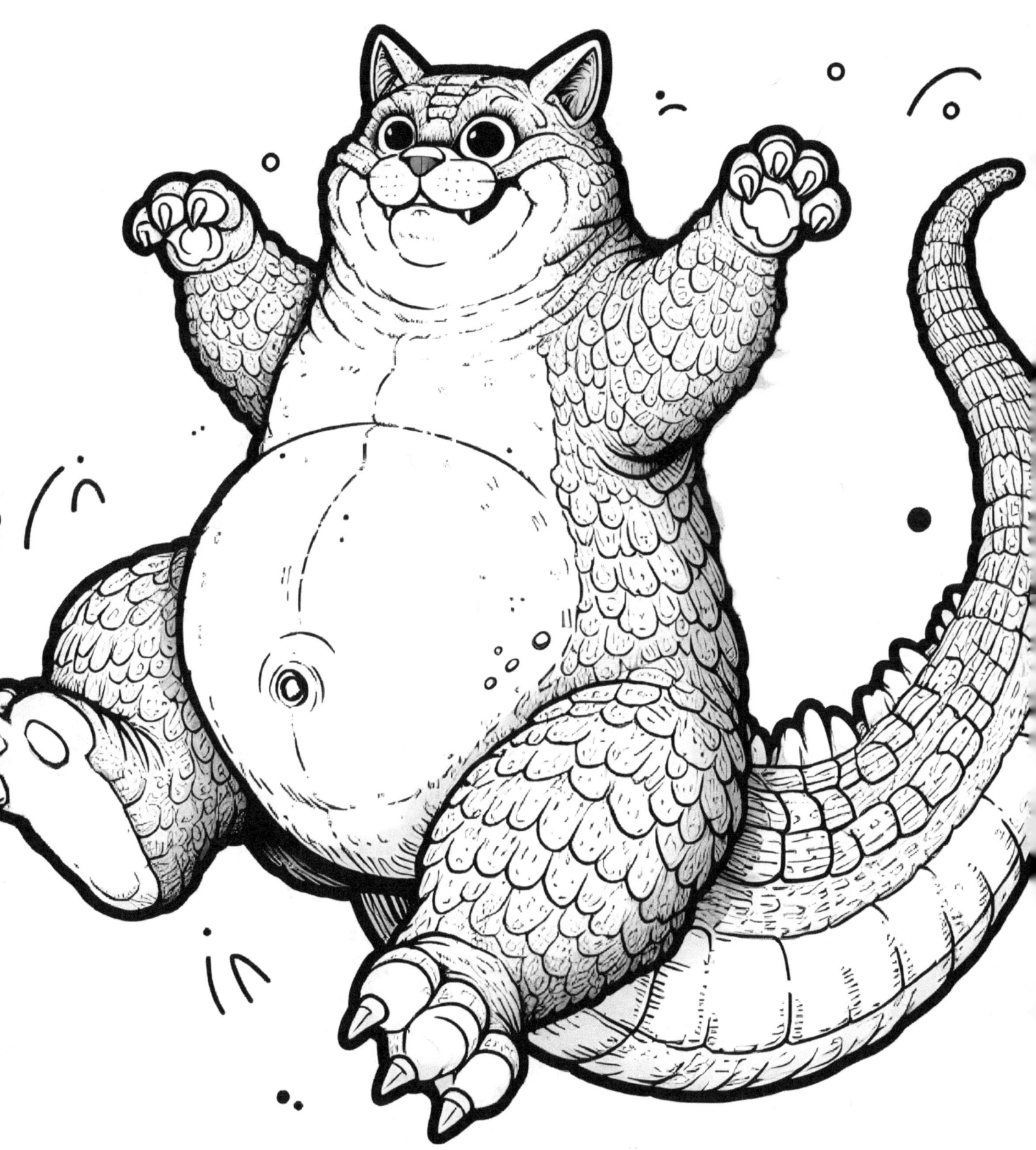

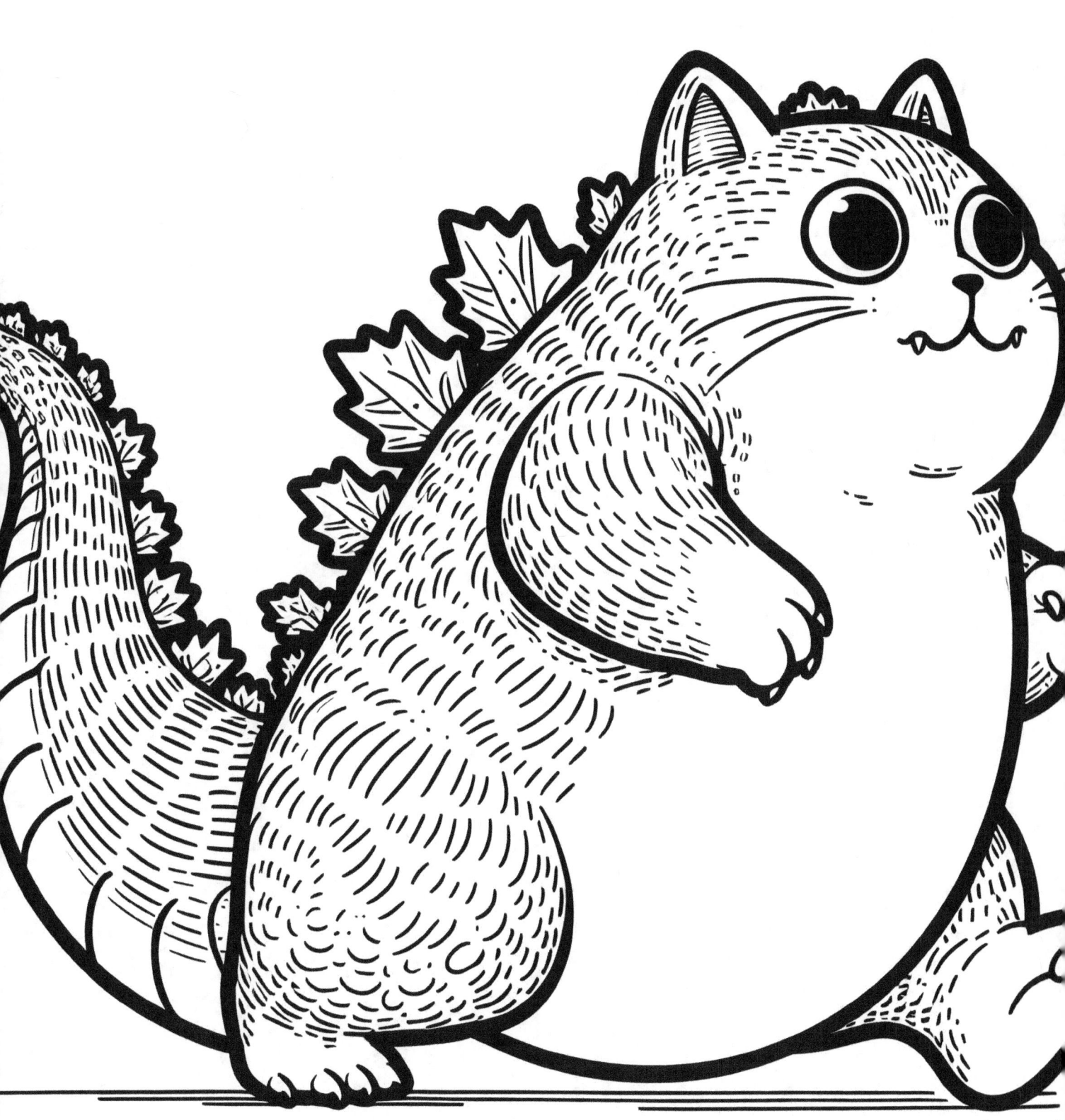

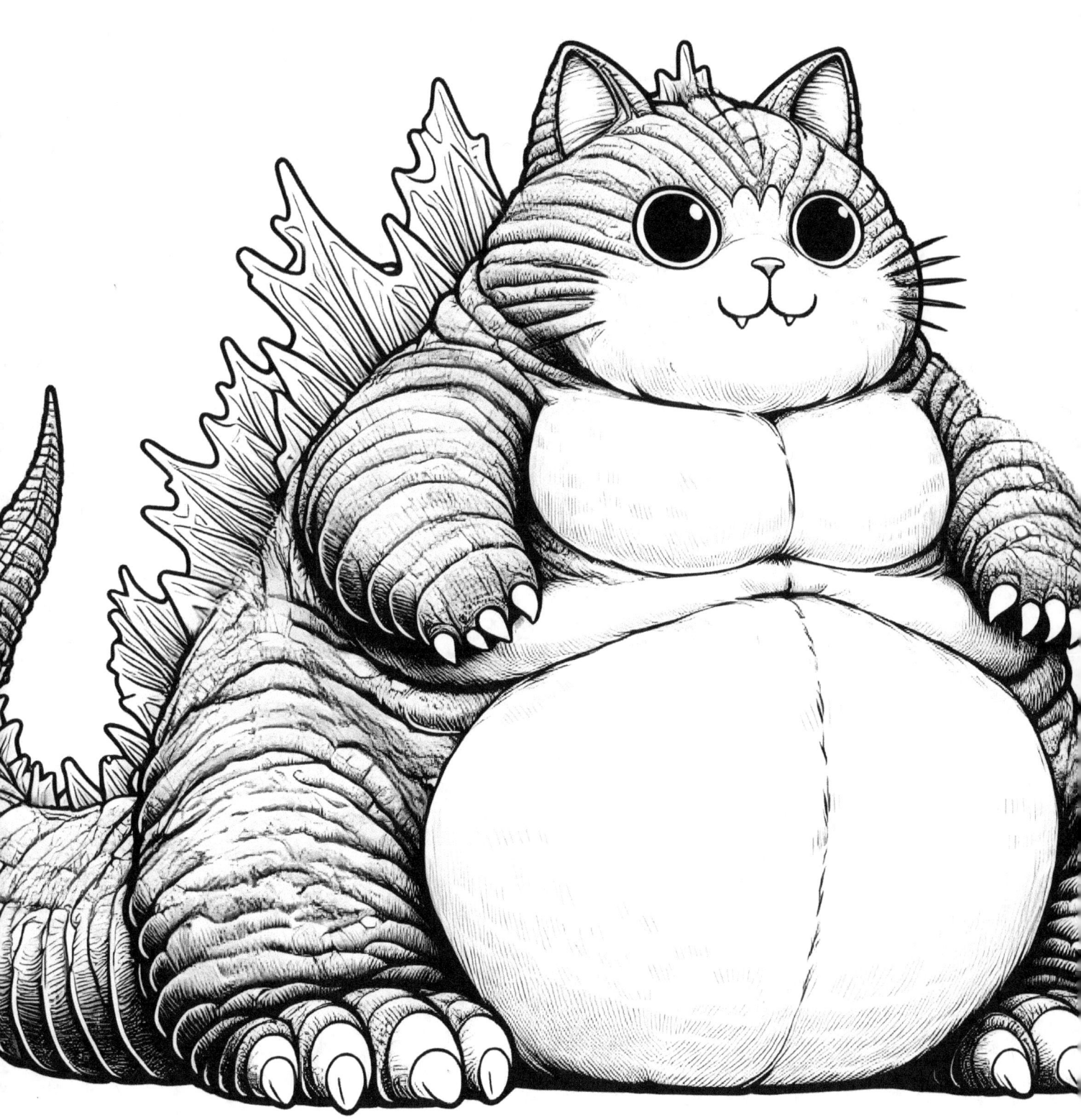

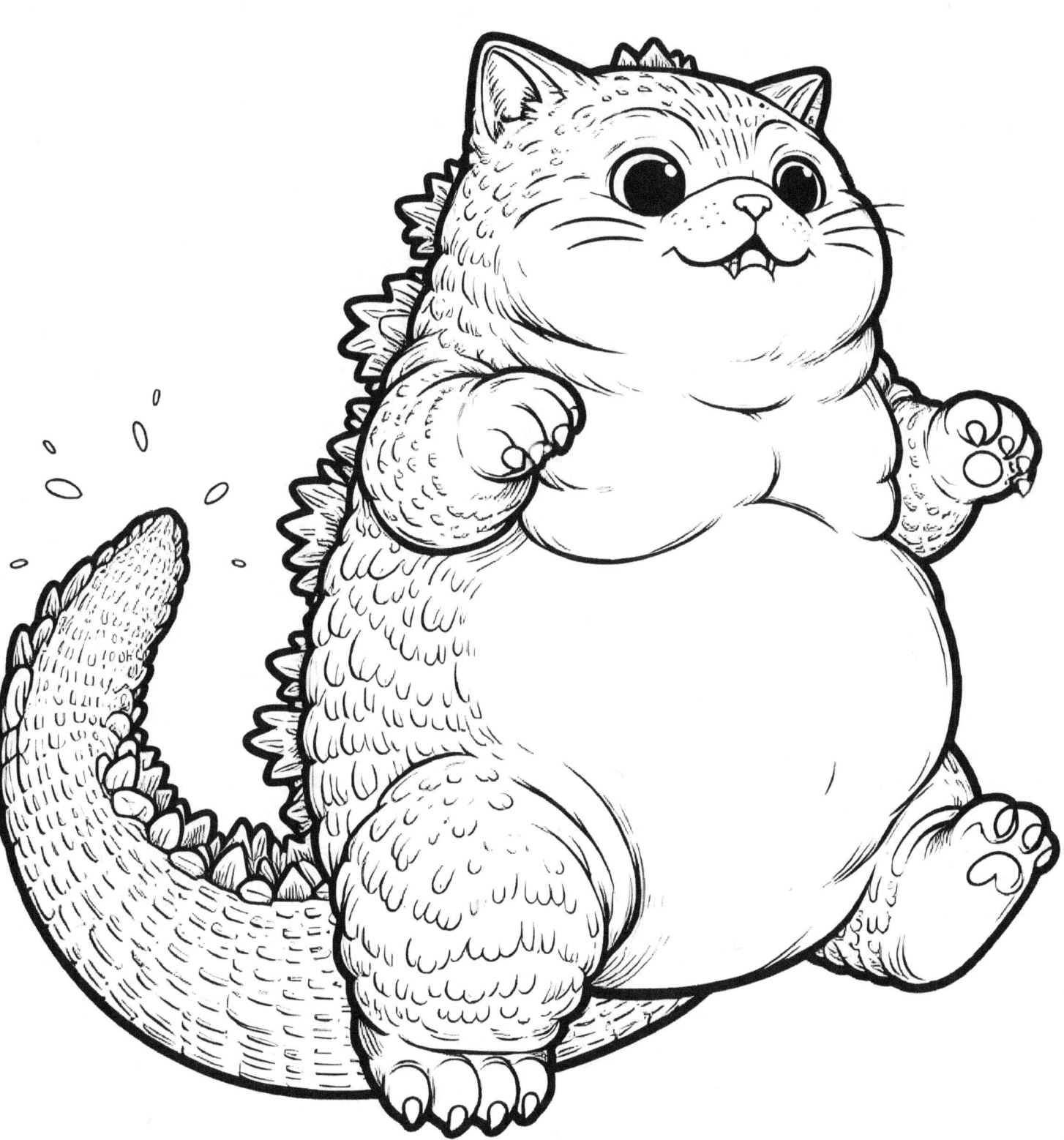

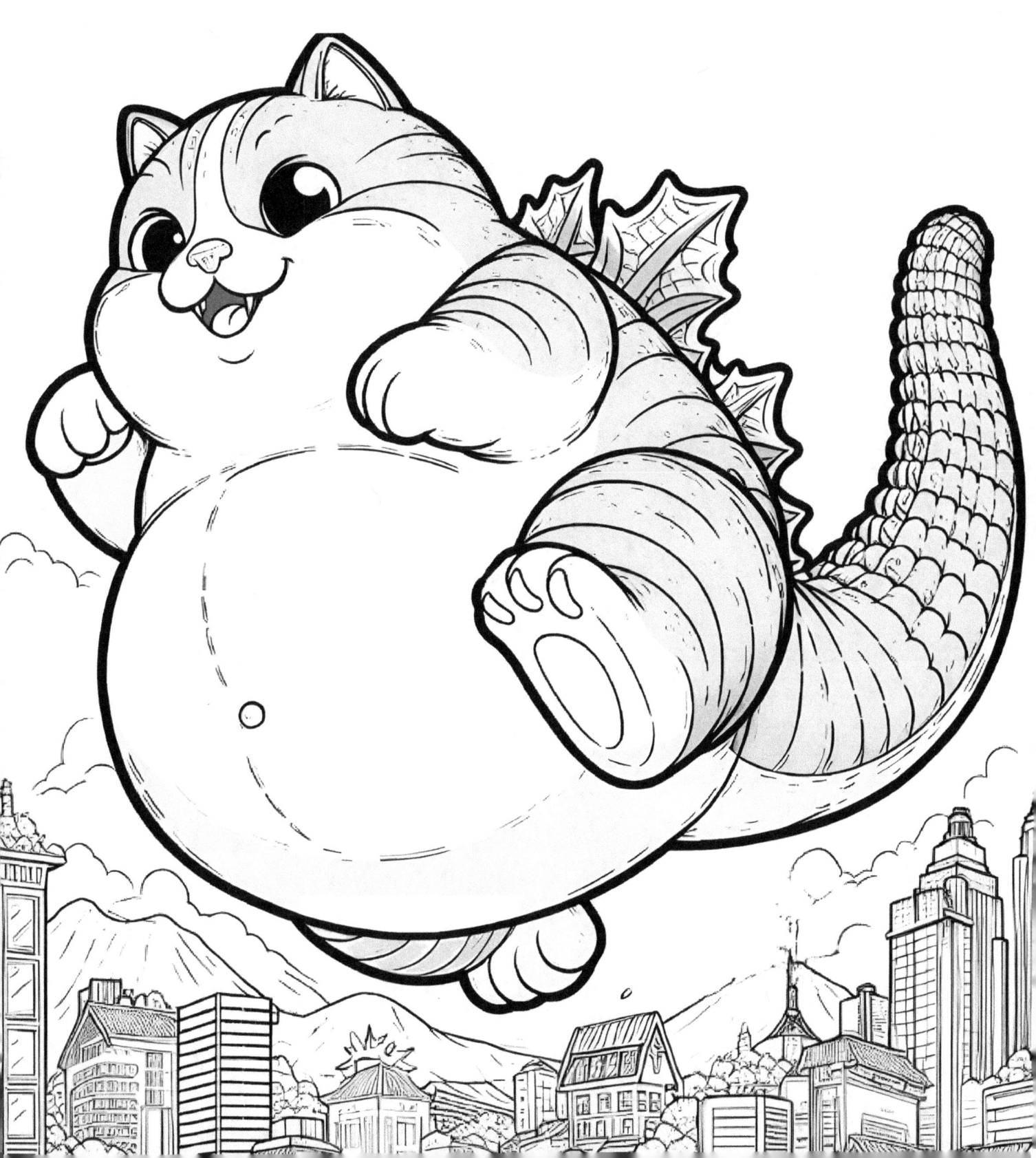

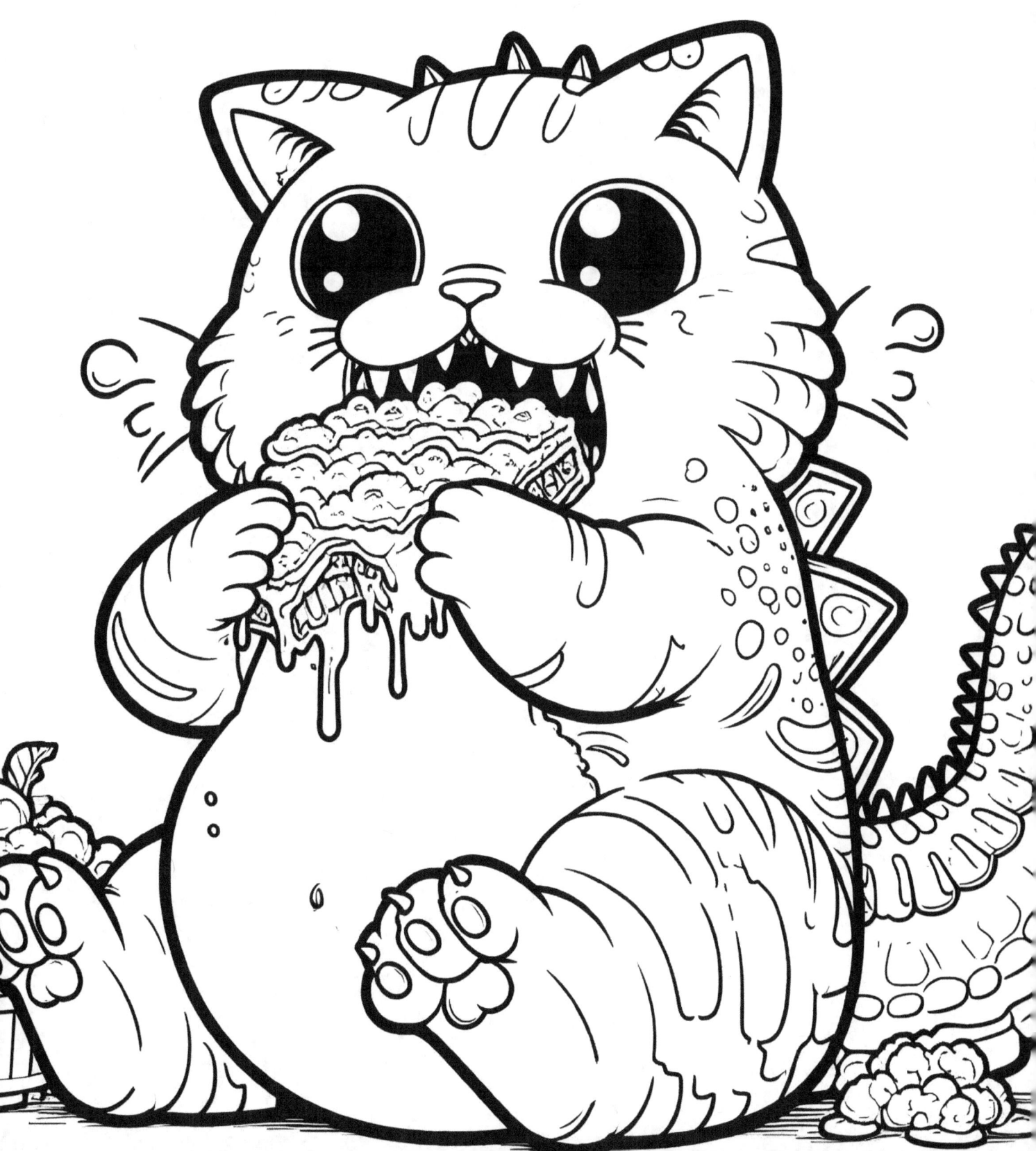

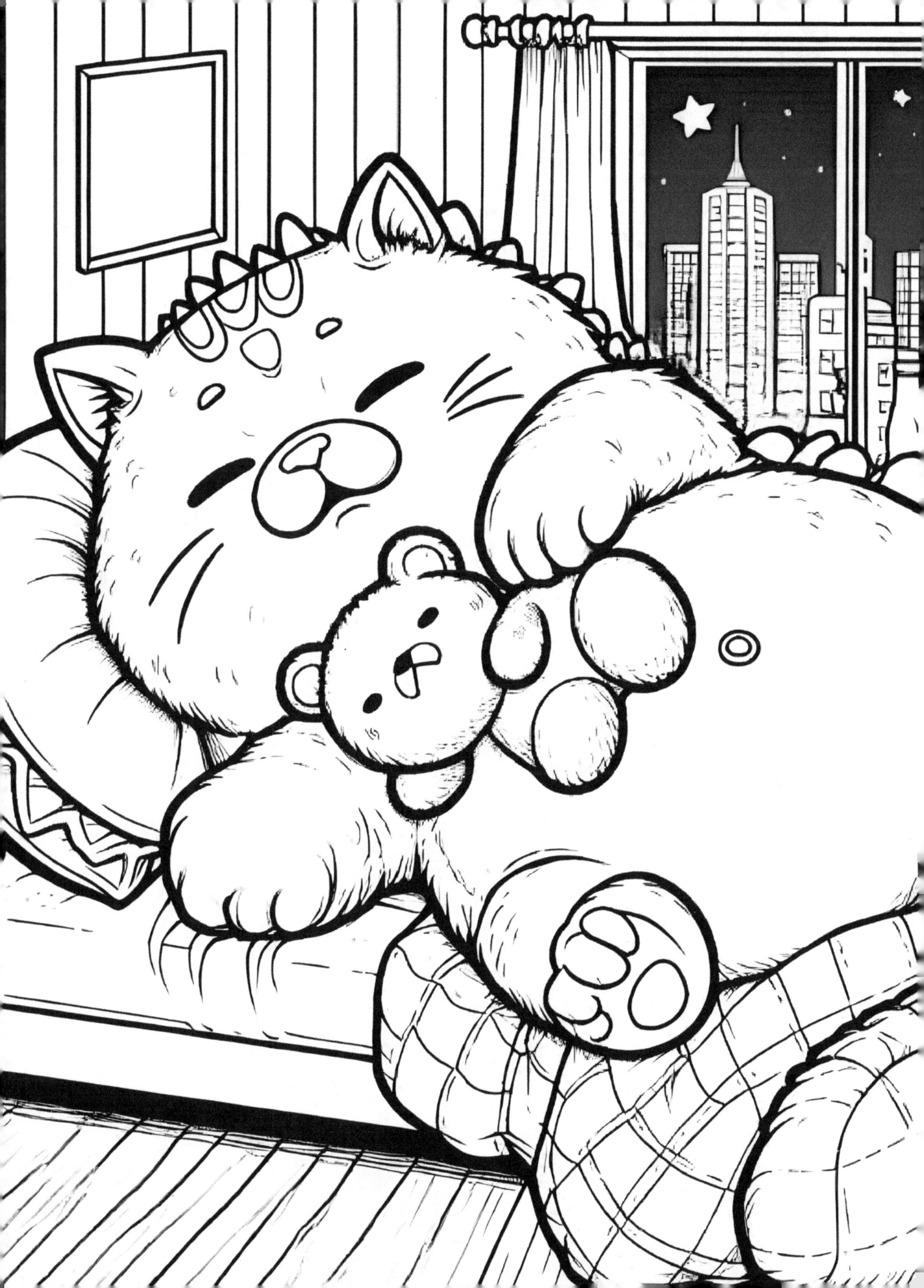

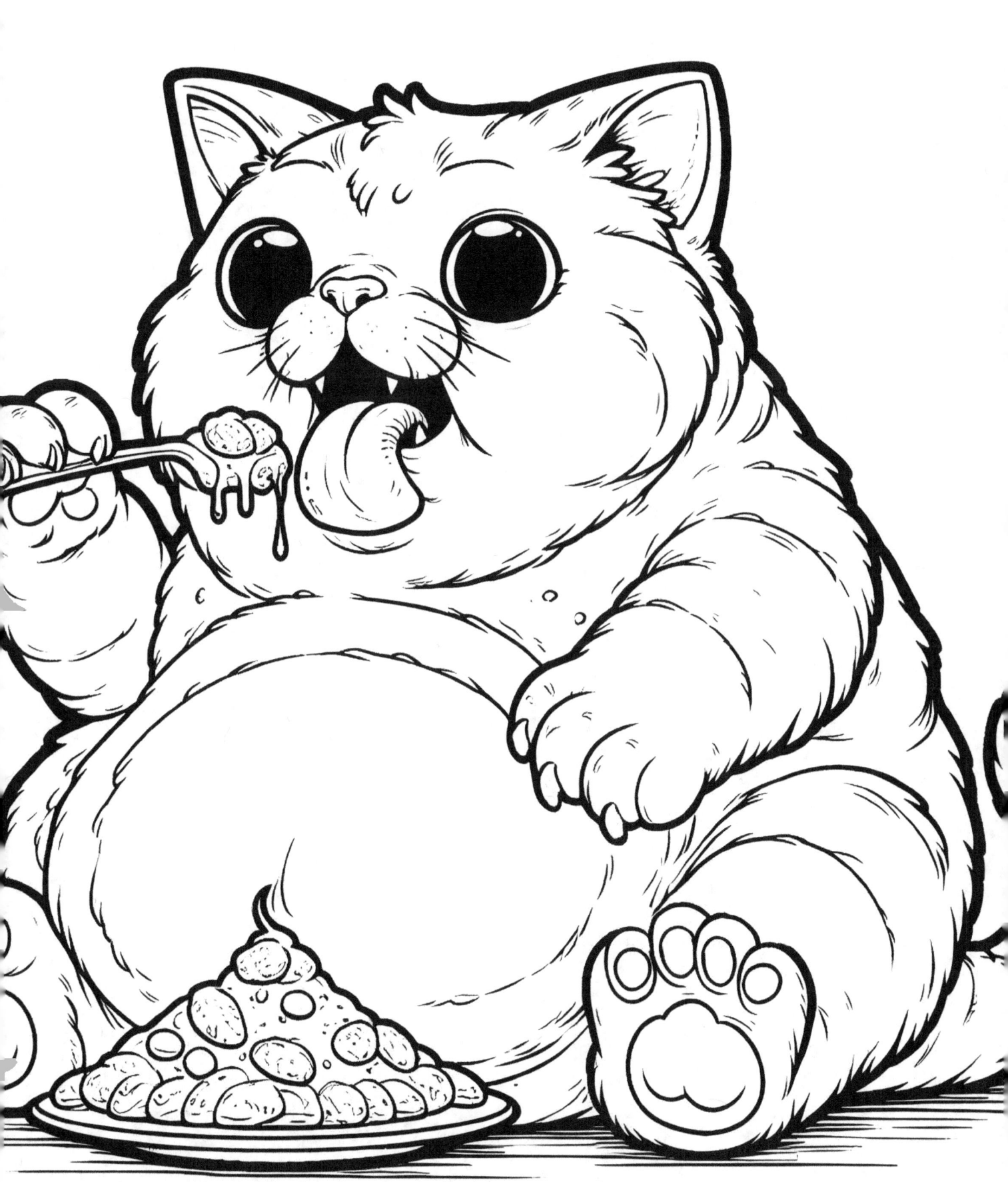

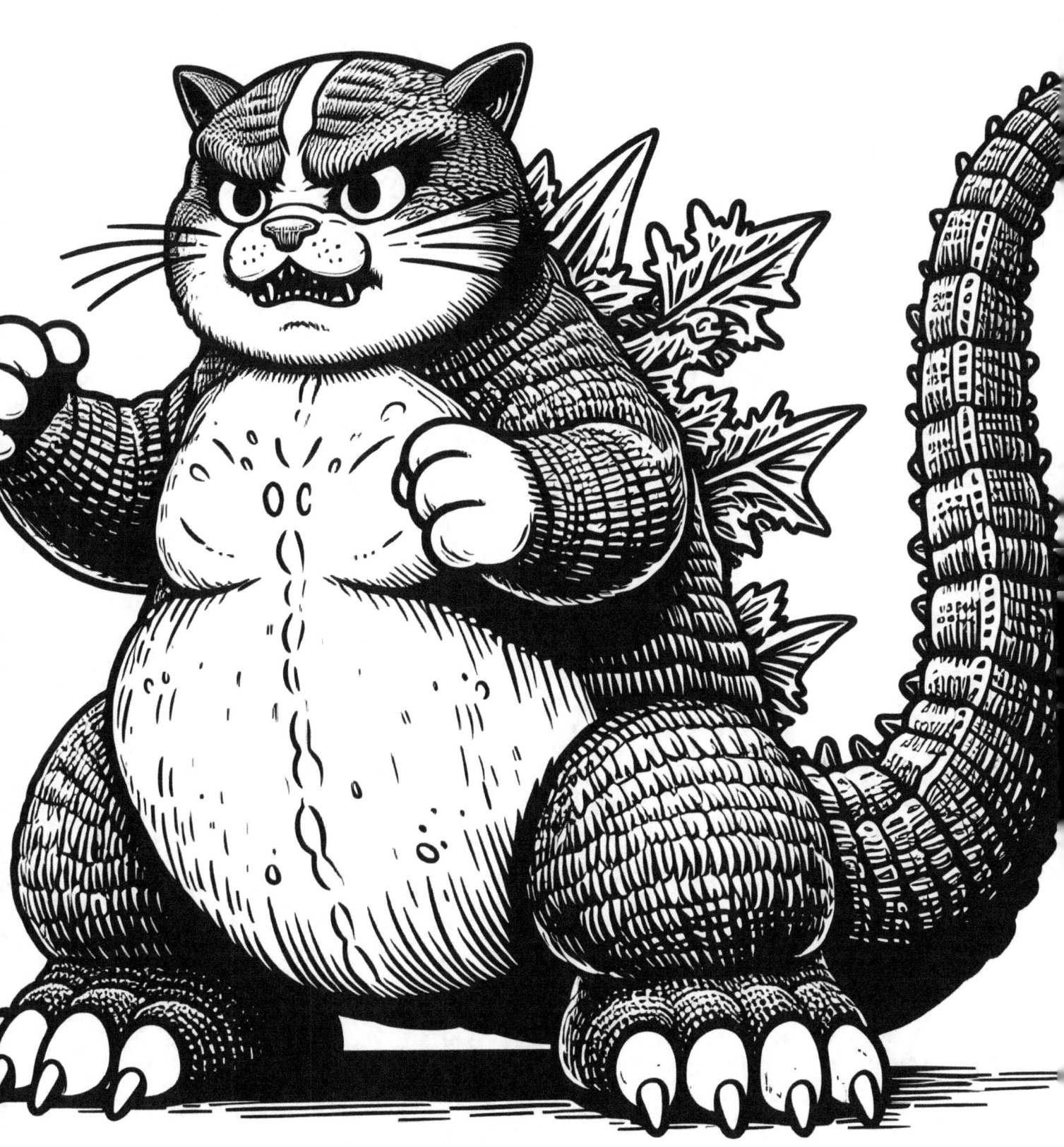

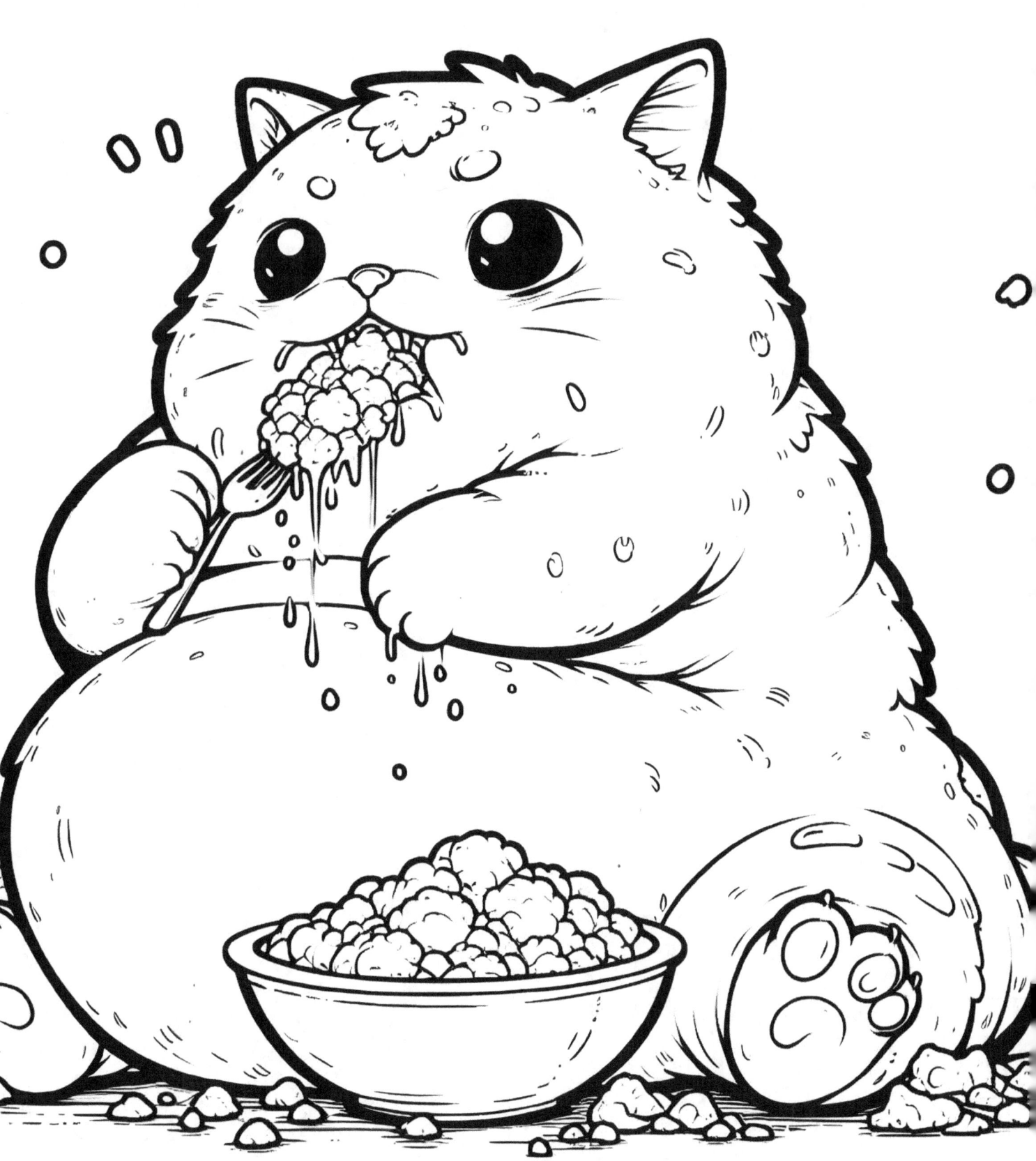

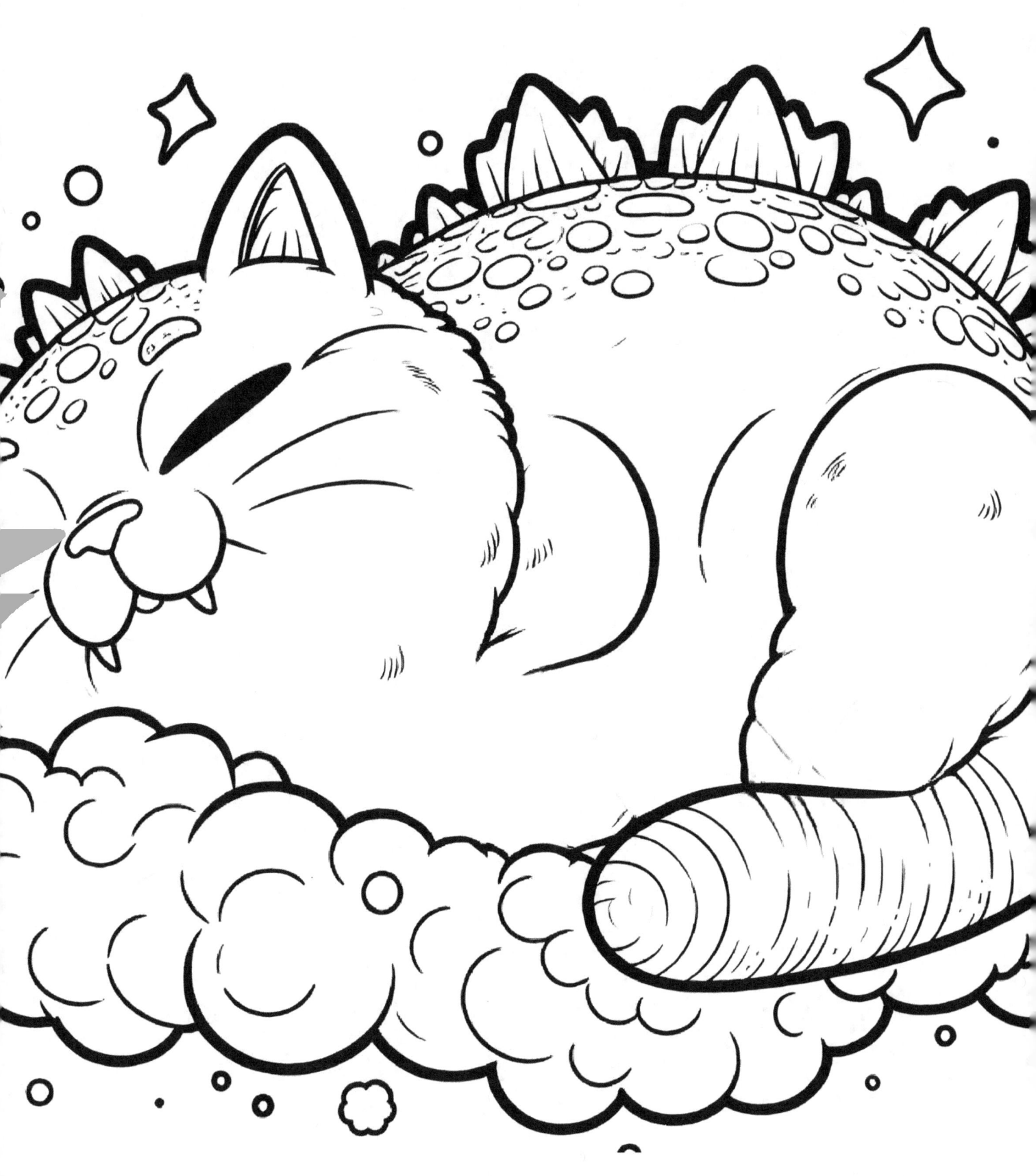

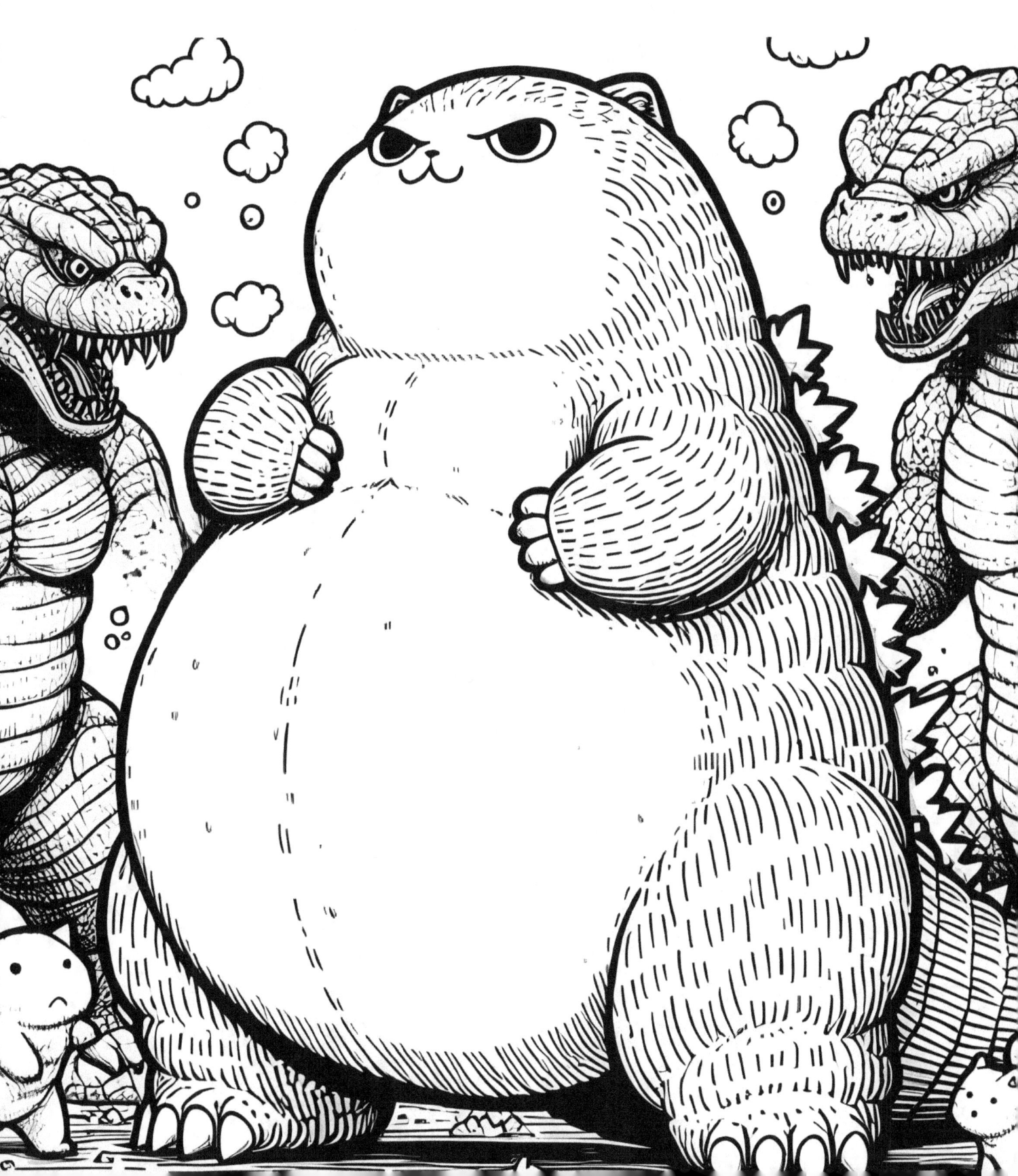

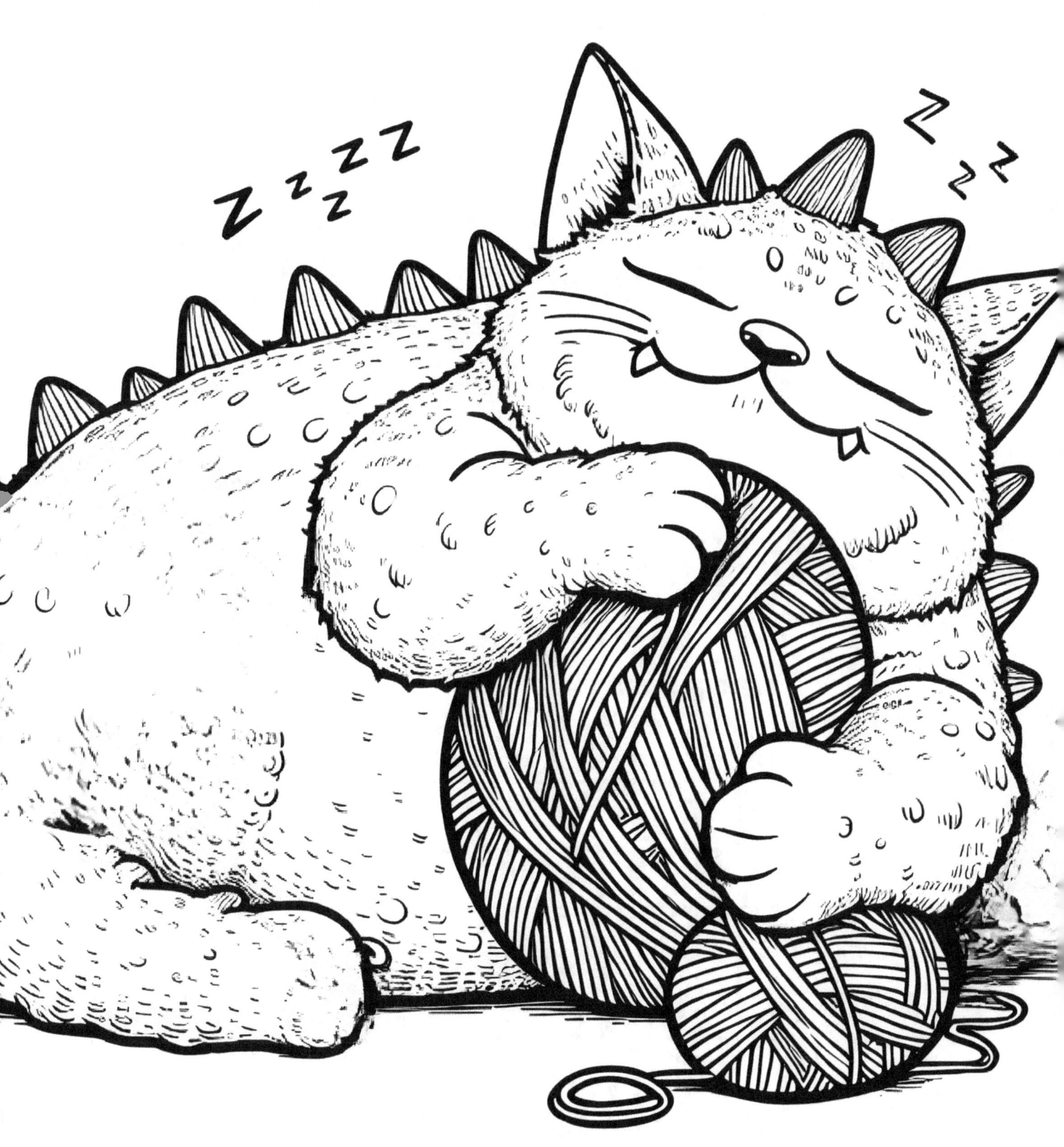

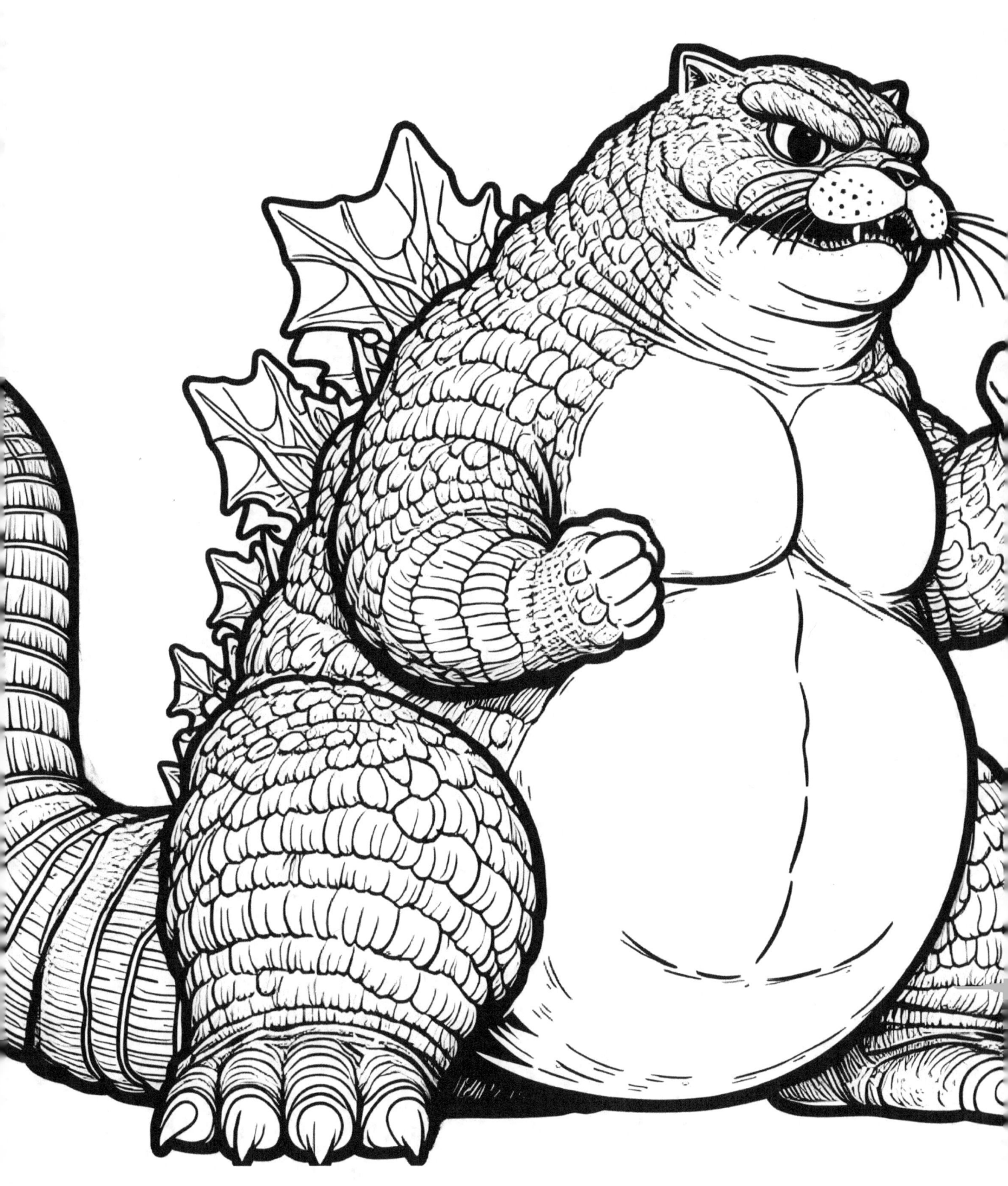

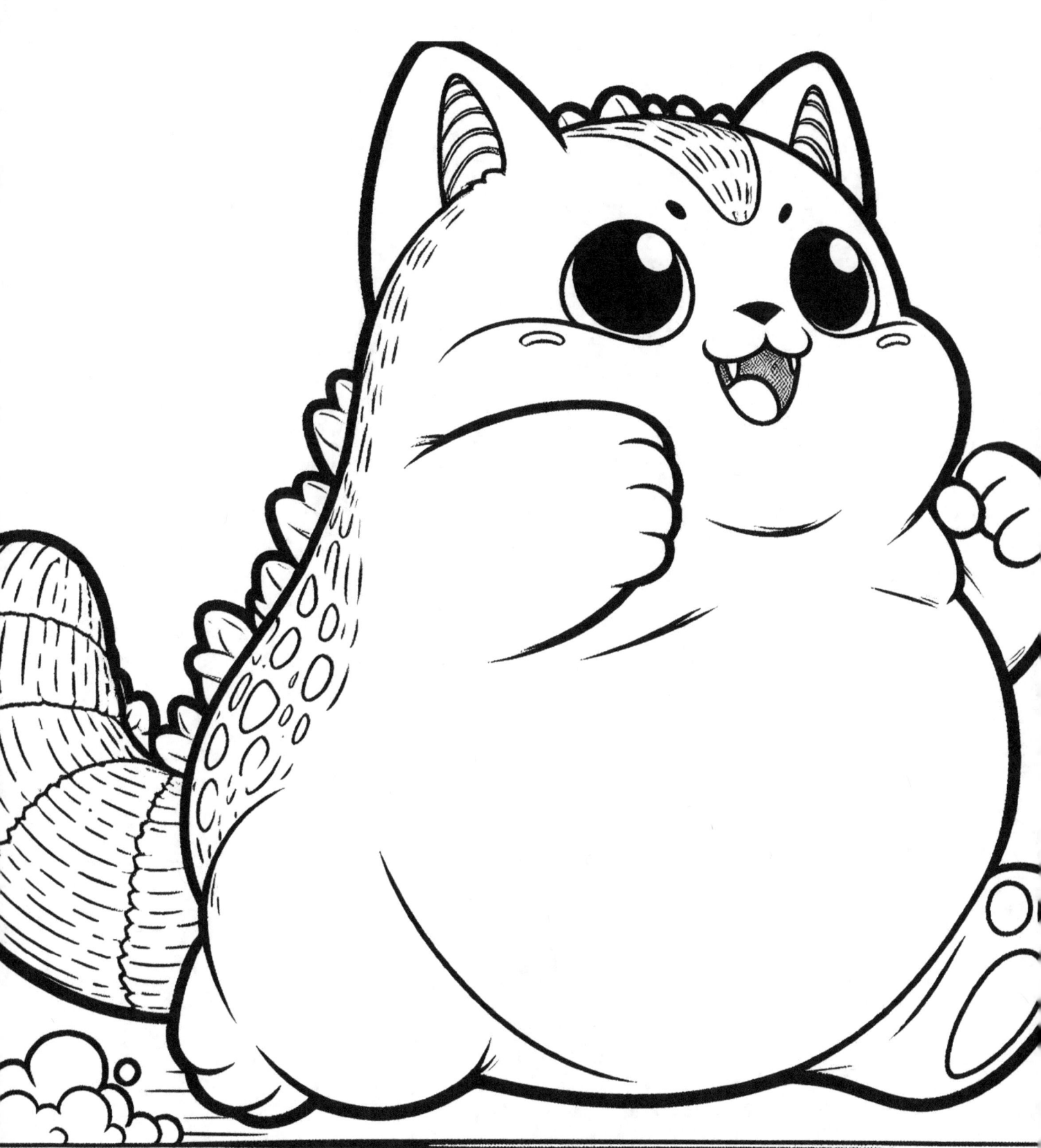

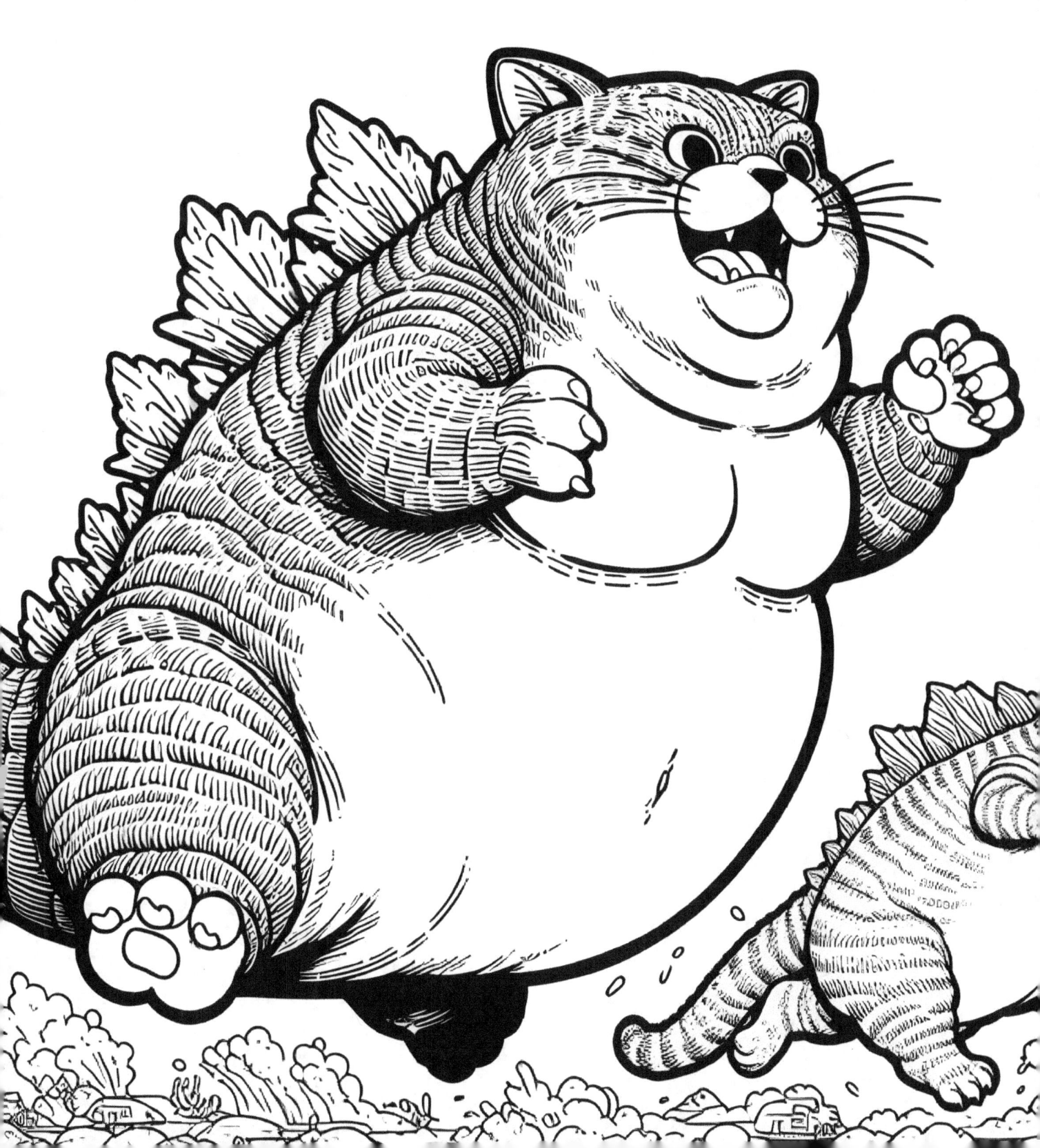

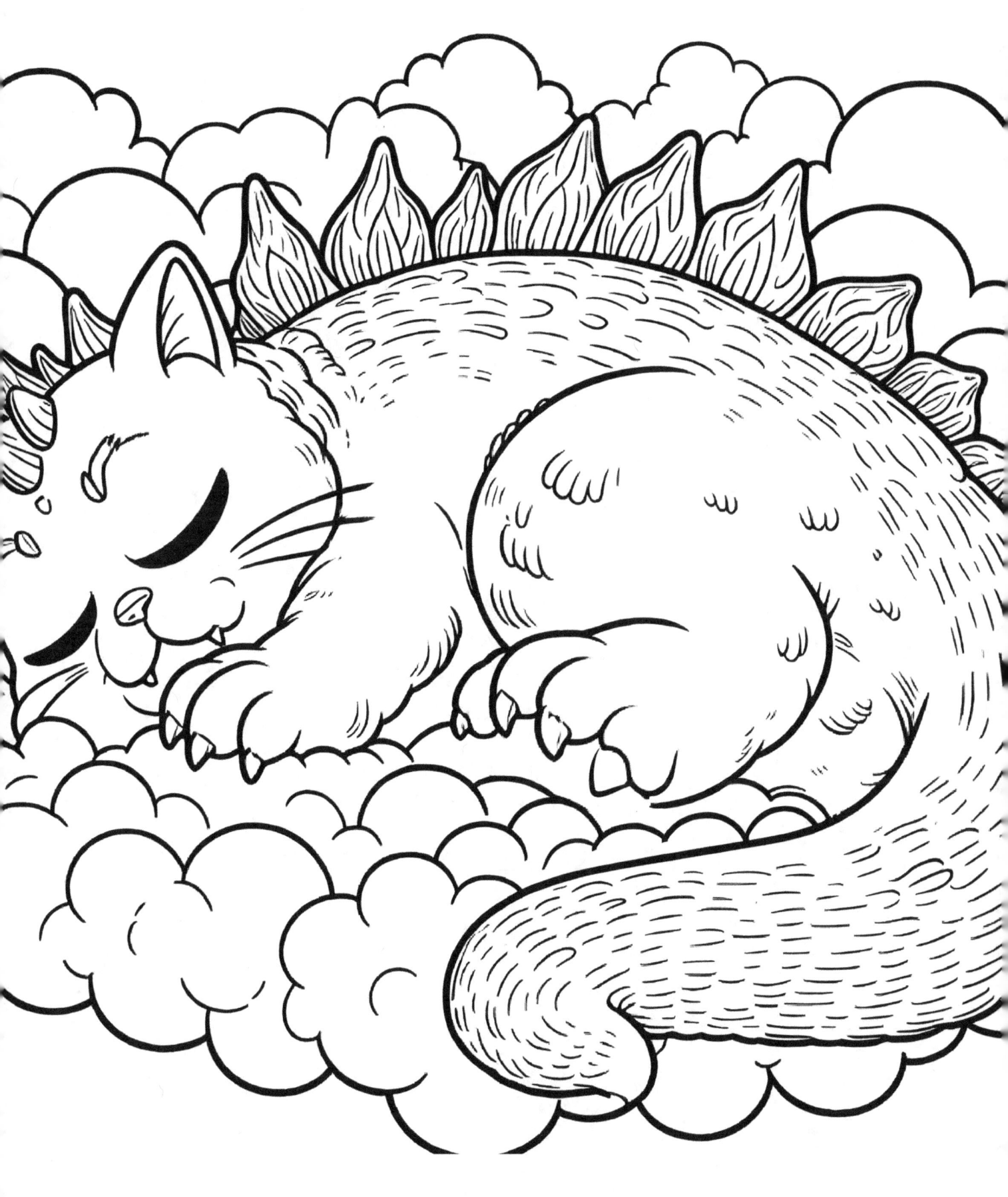

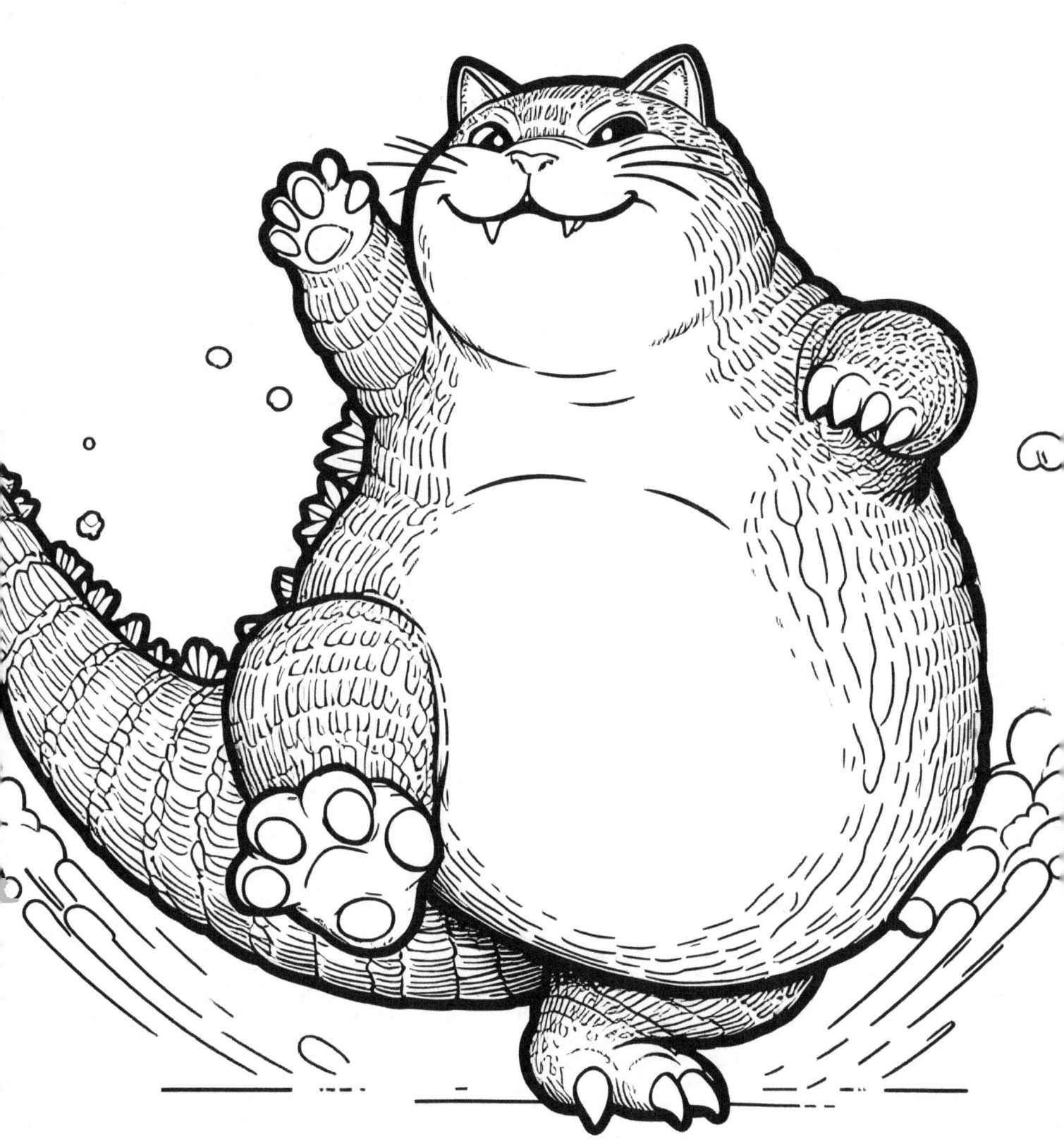

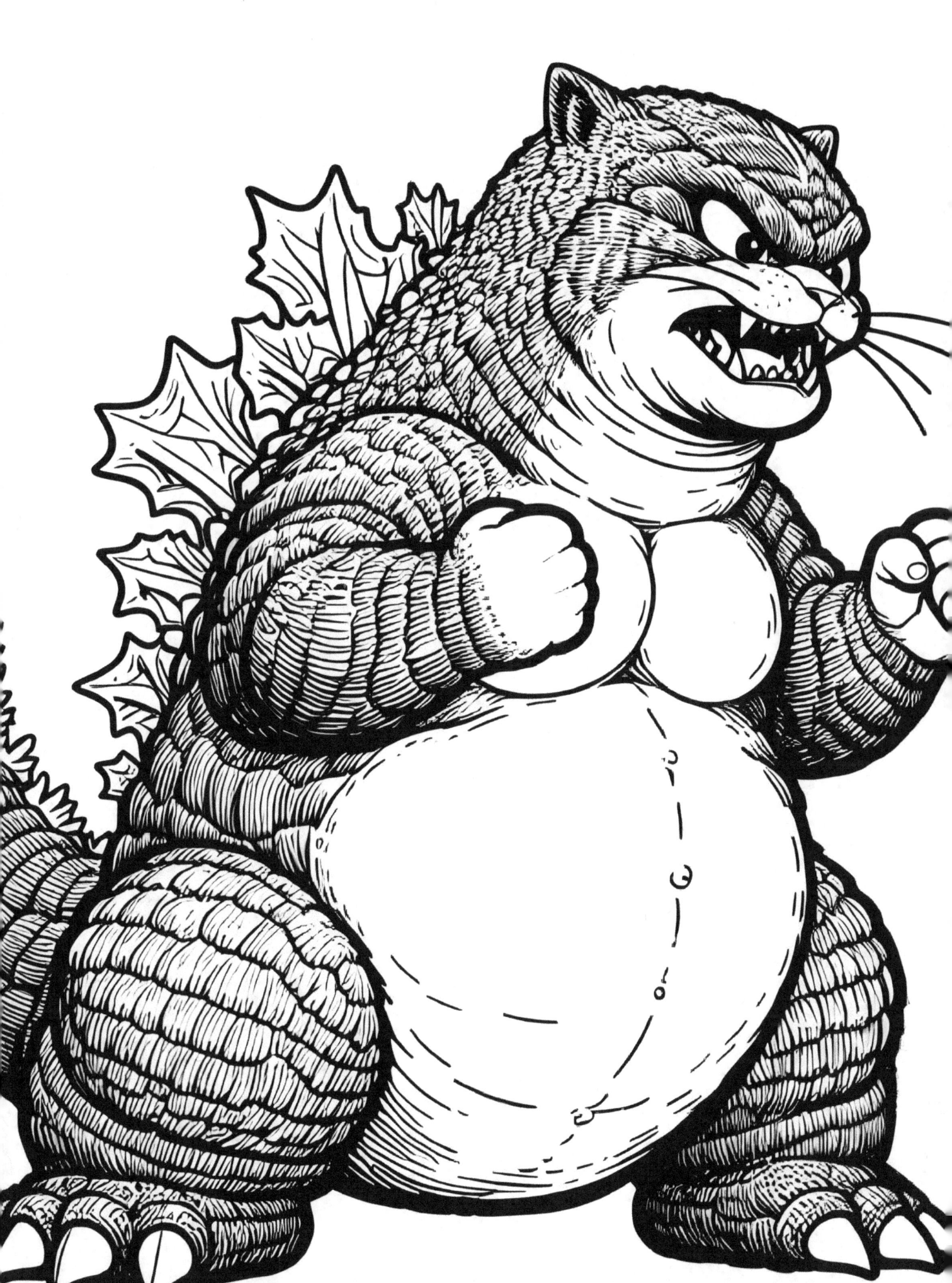

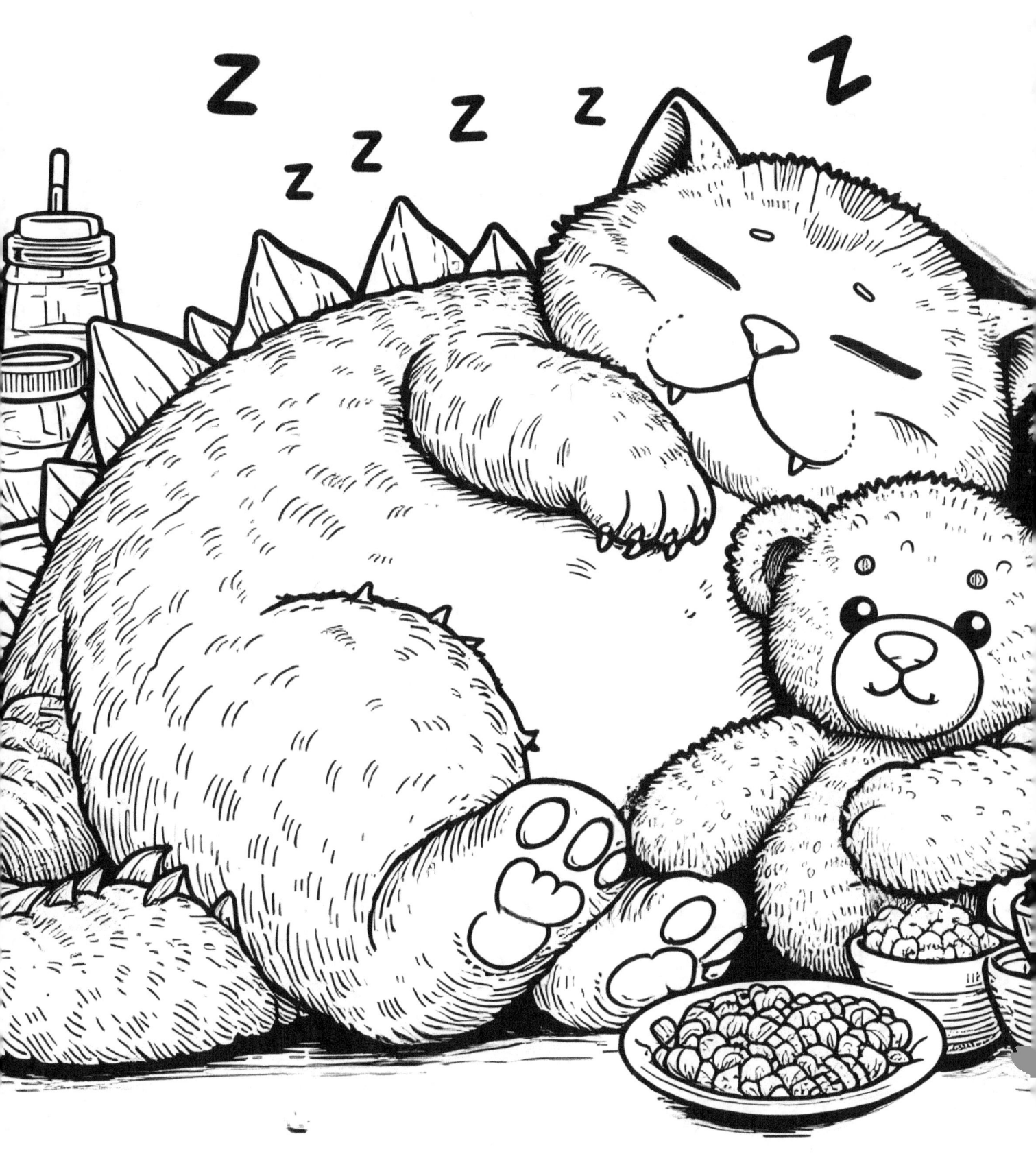

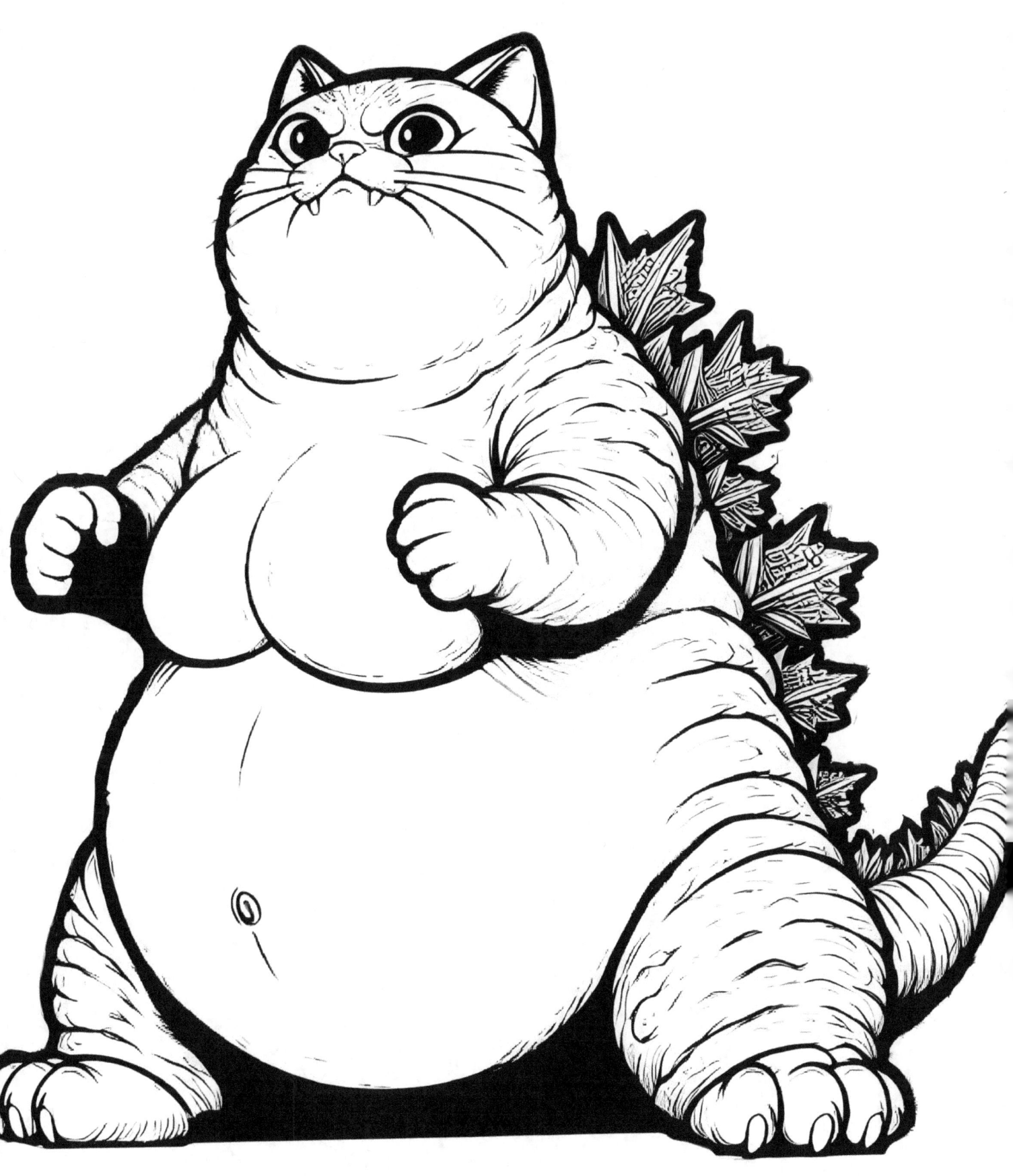

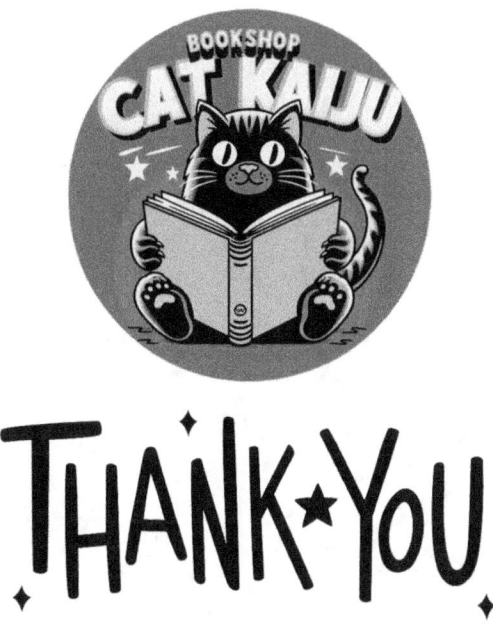

THANK★YOU

For reaching this point with our coloring book from Amazon!

We appreciate your support. If you enjoyed the experience, we'd be grateful if you could leave a review on the Amazon store page.

EXCELLENT BOOK!!

Exciting news! Coming soon: **CatKaiju's official merchandise store!** Get ready to rock CatKaiju gear like never before – from caps and tees to mugs and tote bags, we've got you covered!

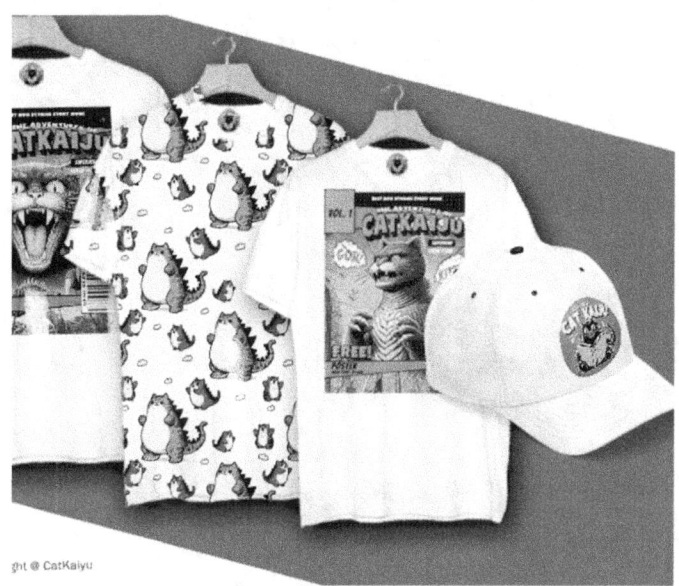

ght @ CatKaiyu

Subscribe to our newsletter for exclusive discounts and be the first to know about our grand opening date and more CatKaiju adventures. Scan the QR code or visit **https://www.catkaiju.shop/newslettersubscription** to subscribe now! Stay tuned for purrfect updates!

www.ingramcontent.com/pod-product-compliance
Lightning Source LLC
Chambersburg PA
CBHW081145290526
45795CB00006B/2375